Green **Line**
Oberstufe Klasse 10

Vorschläge zur Leistungsmessung

von
Victoria Clark
Carolyn Jones
Jon Marks
Dr. Gisela Winkler
Alison Wooder

Ernst Klett Verlag
Stuttgart • Leipzig

Liebe Lehrerin, lieber Lehrer,

die *Green Line Oberstufe Klasse 10* Vorschläge zur Leistungsmessung orientieren sich an den Anforderungen für die Leistungsfeststellung.
Wie Sie wissen, legen die neuen Lehrpläne ganz besonderen Wert auf Kompetenzorientiertheit und kommunikativen Anspruch. Darauf haben wir bei der Entwicklung dieses Hefts geachtet, um Ihnen Aufgabenformate an die Hand zu geben, die auf dem neuesten Stand sind und sich daher optimal für die Erstellung von Klassenarbeiten eignen.
Bei der Entwicklung der kompetenzorientierten Aufgaben wurde besonderer Wert auf die Einbettung in für die Schüler aus dem Alltag bekannte Situationen gelegt.

Aufbau
Im Heft finden Sie Aufgaben zu den sechs Kompetenzen Hörverstehen *(Listening)*, Leseverstehen *(Reading)*, Hör-/Sehverstehen *(Understanding films)*, Schreiben *(Writing)*, Sprechen *(Speaking)* und Sprachmittlung *(Mediation)*. Da Sie alle Aufgaben editierbar auf der Lehrersoftware finden, können Sie diese beliebig und abgestimmt auf das Niveau Ihrer Klasse zu einer Klassenarbeit zusammenstellen. So können z.B. Vorgaben reduziert oder ganz entfernt und Teilaufgaben gewählt werden. Zudem zeigt Ihnen das ⊿-Symbol an, dass es sich um eine vergleichsweise anspruchsvollere Aufgabe handelt.

Für die Speaking-Aufgaben sollte den SchülerInnen Zeit zur Vorbereitung, d.h. zum Lesen der Aufgabe, zur Bildbetrachtung und ggf. dem Anfertigen von Notizen, gegeben werden. Alle Abbildungen der *Speaking*-Aufgaben finden Sie zum Ausdrucken (ggf. farbig) und Laminieren auf der beiliegenden CD-ROM.

Aufgaben zur Abfrage von Wortschatz und Grammatik finden Sie in der Rubrik *Language in use* im zweiten Teil dieses Hefts. Da zunehmend die kommunikative Gesamtleistung des Schülers im Vordergrund steht, ist diese Art von Aufgabe nicht mehr in allen Bundesländern Bestandteil von Klassenarbeiten. Vielmehr sind sie für den Einsatz in kleineren Tests gedacht.

Sollten Sie bislang mit den *Green Line Oberstufe Klasse 10* Standardaufgaben arbeiten, können Sie mit dem vorliegenden Heft *Vorschläge zur Leistungsmessung* nun auf einen erweiterten Aufgabenpool zugreifen.

Wir wünschen Ihnen weiterhin viel Erfolg und Freude bei der Arbeit mit *Green Line*!

Inhalt

Topic 1 Growing up

1 Listening: A book review

Either:

a) *Listen to the book review. Are these statements true or false? Tick (✔) the right box.*

	true	false
1. The book The Dark Before the Dawn is set in Ireland.		
2. Most of the book is about the author's alcoholic father.		
3. Edward preferred the book Angela's Ashes to this book.		
4. Edward says the historical details about the period in the book aren't correct.		
5. The two studio guests have very different opinions of the book.		
6. Tina liked the poetic style of the book.		
7. Tina's main point about the book is that it has a positive, optimistic message.		
8. The author of the book became a jockey in later life.		
9. Tina hopes that the book won't be filmed.		
10. Tina does not think that autobiographies have to be completely truthful.		

b) *Correct the false sentences.*

Or:

Listen to the book review. Tick (✔) the correct endings to the sentences. Only one is correct.

1. The *Dark Before the Dawn* is mostly set …
   a) in the 1930s and 1940s. ☐
   b) in the 1950s ☐
   c) in the early 1990s. ☐

2. The book is mostly …
   a) the story of a boy finding happiness in a difficult childhood. ☐
   b) the story of a boy and his horse. ☐
   c) about how the author became a writer. ☐

3. The main reason Edward disliked the book was because …
   a) he thought it was only written to make money. ☐
   b) he thought that the author had stolen the ideas from another writer. ☐
   c) he doesn't like reading autobiographies. ☐

4. The only positive thing Edward has to say about the book is that …
   a) it deals truthfully with a difficult subject. ☐
   b) the characterization seems quite realistic. ☐
   c) some of the descriptions give a good sense of the period. ☐

5. Tina enjoyed the book because …
   a) she felt it was entirely based on facts. ☐
   b) she found it positive and optimistic. ☐
   c) she liked the descriptions of a country childhood. ☐

6. Tina disagrees with Edward about the fictional aspects of the book …
   a) because she knows that the author kept detailed diaries. ☐
   b) because the dialogues in the book seem so realistic. ☐
   c) because she thinks that all autobiographies are at least partly fictional. ☐

Green Line Oberstufe Klasse 10
ISBN: 978-3-12-560021-8

2 Listening: Summer camp

Either:
A mother and her daughter have very different ideas about summer camps.
Listen and complete the missing information in the table. Use up to four words.

	Elena's view	Elena's mother's view
Accommodation in the summer camp	– in (1) ____________ or very large dormitories with lots of other people	– in a cabin, sharing a nice (2) ____________ with four other girls
Food / kitchen facilities in the camp	– (3) ____________	– meals served in a (4) ____________ or barbecues cooked outdoors
Things to do at the summer camp	– walking in the forest – sports	– walking in the forest – (5) ____________ classes – (6) ____________ workshops
Languages used at the summer camp	– (7) ____________	– many English-speakers
Cost / Finances	– too expensive	– 10% discount for paying early – (8) ____________ will pay

Or:
Listen and complete the answers to these questions.

1. How would Elena travel to the summer camp?

   She would travel ____________

2. How does her mother know that Elena hasn't read the brochure yet?

   The brochure ____________

3. What activities is Elena interested in?

   She's interested in ____________

4. According to her mother, what does Elena spend a lot of her free time doing?

   She spends a lot of time ____________

5. Why will Elena have no difficulties with the language, according to her mother?

   Because Elena ____________

6. When is Elena's mother going to buy Elena's ticket for the summer camp?

   Elena's mother ____________

Green Line Oberstufe Klasse 10
ISBN: 978-3-12-560021-8

3 Reading: Harriet's box of treasures

Harriet came one morning to Emma with a small parcel in her hand, and after sitting down, began:

"I have something that I should like to tell you – a sort of confession to make – and then, you know, it will be over."

Emma was surprised, but begged her to speak. There was a seriousness in Harriet's manner which prepared her for something more than ordinary.

"How could I for so long a time be deceiving myself!" cried[1] Harriet, warmly. "It seems like madness! I can see nothing at all extraordinary in him now. I do not care whether I meet him or not, except that of the two I would rather not see him, and indeed I would go any distance to avoid him. I do not envy his wife in the least. She is very charming, I dare say, and all that, but I think her very bad-tempered and disagreeable[2]! To convince you that I have been speaking the truth, I am now going to destroy what I ought never to have kept, and it is my particular wish to do it in your presence, so that you may see how rational[3] I have become. Cannot you guess what this parcel holds?"

"Not the least in the world. Did he ever give you anything?"

"No, I cannot call them gifts, but they are things that I have valued very much."

She held the parcel towards her, and Emma read the words *Most precious treasures* on the top. Her curiosity was greatly excited. Harriet unfolded the parcel, and she looked on with impatience. Within an abundance[4] of silver paper was a pretty little china box, which Harriet opened. It was well lined with the softest cotton, but, apart from the cotton, Emma saw only a small piece of court plaister[5].

"Now," said Harriet, "you *must* remember,"

"No, indeed I do not."

"Dear me! I should not have thought it possible you could forget what passed in this very room about court plaister! Do not you remember his cutting his finger with your new penknife[6], and your recommending court plaister? But as you had none about you, I took mine out and cut him a piece. But it was a great deal too large, and he cut it smaller, and kept playing some time with what was left, before he gave it back to me. And so then I could not help making a treasure of it, so I put it by[7] never to be used, and looked at it now and then[8] as a great treat."

"My dearest Harriet!" said Emma, "Remember it? Yes, I remember it all now – all, except your saving this relic[9]. Well, go on. What else?"

"Here," continued Harriet, turning to her box again, "here is something still more valuable, I mean that *has been* more valuable, because this is what did really once belong to him, which the court plaister never did."

Emma was quite eager to see this superior treasure. It was the end of an old pencil, the part without any lead[10].

"This was really his," said Harriet. "Do not you remember one morning? No, I dare say you do not. But one morning, I forget exactly the day, he wanted to make a note in his pocket-book. Mr Knightley had been telling him something and he wanted to write it down, but when he took out his pencil, there was so little lead that he soon cut it all away, so you lent him another, and this was left upon the table as good for nothing. But I kept my eye on it and, as soon as I dared, picked it up, and never parted with it again from that moment."

"I do remember it," cried Emma, "I perfectly remember it. Well, go on."

"Oh! That's all. I have nothing more to show you, or to say, except that I am now going to throw them both on the fire, and I wish you to see me do it."

"But, Harriet, is it necessary to burn the court plaister? I have not a word to say for the bit of old pencil, but the court plaister might be useful."

"I shall be happier to burn it," replied Harriet. "It has a disagreeable look to me. I must get rid of[11] everything. There it goes, and there is an end, thank Heaven, of Mr Elton!"

(Extract from *Emma*, by Jane Austen – lightly abridged from the original)

[1]**cried** said in an emotional voice; [2]**disagreeable** unpleasant; [3]**rational** sensible; [4]**abundance** large amount; [5]**court plaister** (archaic) adhesive plaster, used for covering minor cuts; [6]**penknife** a small folding knife for carrying in a pocket; [7]put by keep or store; [8]**now and then** occasionally, sometimes; [9]**relic** object with symbolic or religious importance; [10]**lead** the part of a pencil which writes; [11]**get rid of** throw away

Green Line Oberstufe Klasse 10
ISBN: 978-3-12-560021-8

Jane Austen (1775 – 1817)

British novelist who introduced a new element of realism into the form, and is now considered one of the greatest writers of all time. Her main novels are *Sense and Sensibility* (1811), *Pride and Prejudice* (1813), *Mansfield Park* (1814), *Emma* (1815), *Northanger Abbey* (completed 1803, published posthumously 1817) and *Persuasion* (published posthumously 1817).

Either:
Read the extract from Emma and tick (✔) the correct answer to each question. Only one is correct.

1. What is inside the box that Harriet shows Emma?
   a) A penknife, some silver paper, a piece of plaster and some pencils. ☐
   b) Some cotton, a piece of plaster and a pencil. ☐
   c) A cotton parcel, a pocket-book, a pencil and some silver paper. ☐

2. Why are these objects valuable to Harriet?
   a) Because Mr Elton gave them to her. ☐
   b) Because they belonged to Mr Elton. ☐
   c) Because they are connected with Mr Elton. ☐

3. Why does Harriet show these objects to Emma?
   a) Because she wants to show Emma how sensible she has become. ☐
   b) Because she wants to talk about her love for Mr Elton. ☐
   c) Because she thinks that Emma will be interested in the objects. ☐

4. Why does Harriet decide to get rid of the objects?
   a) Because she now realises how worthless they are. ☐
   b) Because she believes that Emma wants to have them. ☐
   c) Because Mr Elton has married someone else. ☐

5. What does Emma think about Harriet's 'confession'?
   a) It embarrasses her. ☐
   b) She's surprised and amused. ☐
   c) She thinks Harriet is very silly. ☐

6. What does Harriet do with the objects?
   a) She burns them both on the fire. ☐
   b) She puts them back into the box and takes them home. ☐
   c) She burns the pencil but gives the court plaister to Emma. ☐

7. Which of these statements isn't true?
   a) The text is written from the point of view of a third-person narrator. ☐
   b) The writing style is light and humorous. ☐
   c) The author tells the reader exactly what to think about the characters. ☐

Green Line Oberstufe Klasse 10
ISBN: 978-3-12-560021-8

Or:
Is the following information true, false or not in the text?
Tick (✔) the right box.

	true	false	not in text
1. The passage describes a conversation between two young women who know each other well.			
2. Before this conversation, Harriet and Mr Elton had been in love.			
3. Harriet doesn't want to meet Mr Elton again.			
4. Harriet likes the woman that Mr Elton has married.			
5. The piece of court plaister originally belonged to Emma.			
6. Harriet picked up the piece of pencil without Emma or Mr Elton noticing.			
7. Emma thinks Harriet is very silly and immature.			
8. Emma and Harriet are the same age as each other.			
9. Emma and Harriet are of equal intelligence and understanding.			
10. Harriet feels that this conversation marks the end of her interest in Mr Elton.			

Analysis:
Answer the questions.

1. What can you guess about what has happened between Harriet and Mr Elton from this passage?
2. Harriet corrects herself when she is speaking about Mr Elton: "… here is something still more valuable, I mean that has been more valuable, … ." (line 59) What indication does this give about her feelings?
3. Find two descriptions of Emma's feelings about Harriet's confession. What is the effect of these descriptions on the reader?
4. Examine Harriet's language and sentence structure. Explain the effect her style of speech has on the reader.
5. Describe the narrative effects the author uses to create a comic effect in this passage. Give examples from the text to support your views.
6. What is your personal impression of this passage? What does it suggest about the idea of growing up?

Green Line Oberstufe Klasse 10
ISBN: 978-3-12-560021-8

4 Reading: The adolescent brain

Paragraph 1:

Adults often find the behaviour of teenagers hard to understand – and vice-versa, of course. It now appears that this incomprehension may be due to neurobiology[1] rather than just different ways of looking at the world. New findings show that major changes to the parts of the brain that are responsible for functions such as self-control, judgement, emotions and organisation take place during adolescence and continue into early adulthood.

Paragraph 2:

Until recently it was generally believed that the development of the human brain was completed by the early teen years or even before. By the age of six, the brain is 95% of its adult size, and grey matter (the 'thinking' part of the brain) reaches its maximum size at around age 11 for girls and 12 for boys. However, research using magnetic resonance imaging (MRI) technology suggests that the structure of the brain continues to change well into a person's twenties. Most significantly, it seems that the area of the brain responsible for reasoning and problem-solving is the last part to fully develop.

Paragraph 3:

From age 12 the amount of grey matter starts to get smaller. The cells and connections that are used regularly survive and get stronger, while those that are not used die off. In other words, "use it or lose it". The process makes the brain more efficient, as the distracting[2] non-useful connections are gradually discarded[3]. This may explain what to adults can seem irrational[4] and over-emotional behaviour in teenagers. Their thought-processes are easily overwhelmed[5] with irrelevant[6] information. Imagine trying to read a difficult poem in a quiet library (adult thought process) and in a crowded, noisy café (teenage thought process). Cool, calm analysis is simply not something the teenage brain is physically able to do very well.

Paragraph 4:

The findings have much greater significance than helping a mother to understand why her 15-year-old daughter keeps getting angry about nothing. The structure of the brain is permanently formed during this period from early teens to early-twenties: skills and abilities are hard-wired[7] for the rest of a person's life. The principle applies to everything from socialising and dancing to mathematics and essay-writing. The 14-year-old who wants to be good at computer programming, acting or painting had better start soon – not beginning until a couple of years from now may be leaving it too late.

Paragraph 5:

Could the results of this research affect the expectations adults have of young people? Is it really fair to expect teenagers to make important choices about their future lives and careers, for example? It also raises questions about the way education is structured. Should school subjects be taught in a different order to match the development of the brain? Are schools and teachers doing enough to help their students develop life-long abilities? Should lessons be more about problem-solving and decision-making and less about memorising facts? It's reasonable for teenagers to expect parents, teachers and schools to give them as good a start in life as possible, and now there's some new evidence[8] on the table.

[1]**neurobiology** the biology of the brain; [2]**distracting** spoiling mental concentration; [3]**discarded** thrown away; [4]**irrational** not logical; [5]**overwhelmed** given too much; [6]**irrelevant** unimportant, not useful; [7]**hard-wired** permanently fixed; [8]**proof** important information

Either:

Find the correct sub-headings to the five paragraphs. There is one more heading than you need.

A: The brain gradually becomes more efficient. ____

B: Time to rethink educational policy? ____

C: Don't delay learning life skills ____

D: Research may explain misunderstandings ____

E: Brain development stops at adolescence ____

F: Post-adolescent brain development ____

Green Line Oberstufe Klasse 10
ISBN: 978-3-12-560021-8

Or:
Is the following information true, false or not in the text?
Tick (✔) the right box.

	true	false	not in text
1. There's no scientific reason for behaviour differences between teenagers and adults.			
2. By the time we're around twelve years old, the human brain has finished developing.			
3. The new findings are based on evidence from MRI brain scans.			
4. Teenagers' brains have fewer connections and less grey matter than adult brains.			
5. Adolescent brains have to process more information than adult brains.			
6. Adults are better at interpreting emotional behaviour in other people.			
7. It becomes more difficult to think analytically and unemotionally in adult life.			
8. Teenagers who learn practical skills in adolescence are likely to get better jobs.			
9. Skills are learned better in adolescence than in adulthood.			
10. The new findings could change the way teenagers are educated in the future.			

Analysis:
Answer the questions.

1. According to this article, how is teenage behaviour typically regarded by adults? Find two phrases in the article which describe traditional views of adolescent behaviour and thinking.

2. In your own words, complete these sentences by summarizing the argument in the second paragraph of the article:
   – It was generally believed that …
   – It now appears that …

3. Summarize what happens to the human brain from the age of twelve to the early twenties.

4. In the third paragraph, what stylistic device does the writer use to compare adult thought processes with teenage thought processes? What is the effect of this device?

5. Explain the importance of timing for learning life skills.

6. Summarize the author's opinions of why these findings are important.

7. What are your own views of the subject of this article? Should education be organized differently? If so, what differences should there be?

Green Line Oberstufe Klasse 10
ISBN: 978-3-12-560021-8

5 Understanding films: Discrimination

a) *Watch the news item and tick (✔) the correct answer to each question. Only one is correct.*

1. Who is calling on the government to do more to stop black men from being victimised?
   a) The BBC. ☐
   b) A committee of MPs[1]. ☐
   c) The police. ☐

2. Which of these findings was mentioned in the report?
   a) The number of arrests of young black men has grown by 300% in recent years. ☐
   b) Far more crimes are committed by young white men than by young black men. ☐
   c) Far more young black men than young white men are stopped and searched by the police. ☐

3. Which of these statistics does Clare Marshall quote from the report?
   a) 75% of the young black men will soon be on the DNA data base. ☐
   b) More than 50% of British young black men have been arrested recently. ☐
   c) Nearly 66% of young black men will be stopped and searched this year. ☐

4. According to the news item, who is to blame for the fact that so many young black men are arrested or stopped and searched?
   a) The police. ☐
   b) There is no agreement on one likely cause for the problem. ☐
   c) The young men and their families. ☐

5. What does Claudia Webb think that the report shows?
   a) More needs to be done to fight crime. ☐
   b) Young black people need to take more responsibility for their actions. ☐
   c) Young black people are treated unfairly. ☐

6. What is the main purpose of this piece of journalism?
   a) To investigate the effects of crime. ☐
   b) To discuss a new report and the questions it raises. ☐
   c) To educate young black men. ☐

[1] **MP** Member of Parliament

b) *Analyze the video by answering the following questions.*

1. According to the studio presenter, what is the main point made by the report?
2. Explain what the outreach group in Peckham, South London, is trying to do.
3. According to the police officer, what is the reaction of the police to the report?
4. What people are blamed by the young men, the boy, and Claudia the consultant?
5. Explain what Claudia Webb means when she says 'I think this is institutionalised racism'.
6. Several different people and places are featured in the report. What is the effect of showing a variety of speakers and locations?

Green Line Oberstufe Klasse 10
ISBN: 978-3-12-560021-8

6 Writing: An article

Write an article for your school magazine discussing the topic of the cartoon. Include your own personal opinions. Write about 150 words.

- Present the situation shown in the cartoon.
- Interpret the message the cartoonist wishes to convey.
- Do you think the message is true to real life? Explain why / why not.

© Mike Baldwin / Cornered

"With a good education you can grow up to be anything I want you to be."

7 Writing: A speech

Average unemployment rates across the EU, January 2012	
Total, all EU:	10.1% (approx. 24.5 million)
Youth (i.e. below age 25), all EU:	22.4% (approx. 5.5 million)
Highest youth unemployment rate:	Spain, 49.9%
Estimated cost of youth unemployment:	€2 billion per week

Europäische Union, 1995–2012

Write a speech in which you argue that more money should be spent on creating jobs for young people. Write about 150 words.

- Present the situation shown in the statistics.
- Interpret the results of the statistics. What are the effects of this situation?
- Suggest at least one way to improve the situation.

Green Line Oberstufe Klasse 10
ISBN: 978-3-12-560021-8

8 Speaking: A discussion

Part 1: Interview:

1. What kinds of things do you do when you are with friends?
2. How much time do you spend using a mobile phone?
3. What are the most important things in your life at the moment?
4. What are your plans for the future?

Part 2: Individual long turn

Student A: *Describe the first picture and comment on it.*

Student B: *Describe the second picture and comment on it.*

Picture 1

Picture 2

Part 3: Discussion

Student A: *In your opinion, the boy in the second picture is probably just as happy with his life as the teenagers in the first picture are with theirs.*

Student B: *You disagree. In your opinion, the boy in the second picture isn't as happy with his life as the teenagers in the first picture are with theirs.*

Green Line Oberstufe Klasse 10
ISBN: 978-3-12-560021-8

9 Speaking: A discussion

Part 1: Interview:

1. How important is fashion for you?
2. What do you like and / or dislike about current youth fashions?
3. Why do you dress in the style that you do?
4. What would you buy if you won a lot of money to spend on clothes?

Part 2: Individual long turn

Student A: *Describe pictures 1 and 2 and comment on them.*

Student B: *Describe pictures 3 and 4 and comment on them.*

Picture 1

Picture 2

Picture 3

Picture 4

Part 3: Discussion

Student A: *You think youth fashion is a waste of time and money, and you agree with people who criticize it.*

Student B: *You don't think youth fashion is a waste of time and money, and people who criticize it are wrong.*

Green Line Oberstufe Klasse 10
ISBN: 978-3-12-560021-8

10 Mediation: A summary

You're having trouble with your parents because they can't understand why you always get up late at weekends. You've found the article below on the Internet.
As your parents don't speak much English, you summarize the main arguments of the article for them in German.

Wake up, adults – teenagers need more sleep!

The idea that adolescents who like to sleep late on Saturday morning are just lazy has been disproved by medical research. While the ideal amount of sleep for adults is around eight hours per night, adolescents need nine to nine-and-half hours. However, just going to bed earlier won't solve the problem.

A person's sleep / wake cycle is controlled by a process called the circadian rhythm, also known as the "body clock". This makes a person feel sleepy in the evening and makes them wake up in the morning. It's controlled by a chemical produced in the body called melatonin. Adolescents' bodies produce melatonin at different times of the day to adults' bodies, and in particular, the signal to start feeling sleepy tends to happen much later in the day than it does for adults. This explains why it's common for teenagers to be lying awake unable to sleep at 2 a.m., and why it can then be so difficult for them to jump out of bed feeling lively at 7 a.m.

Studies show that in the USA adolescent students get an average of just 6.5 hours sleep on school nights. Most adolescents are sleep-deprived due to the inability to fall asleep until late at night, as described above, plus the pressures of early starts to the school day, homework, family life and social life.

The results of long-term sleep-deprivation can be very serious. It can affect memory and creativity, making it difficult for sleep-deprived students to learn. It can cause stress, lack of self-confidence and depression. Not getting enough sleep can even make a person more likely to become ill.

What can be done? Parents may need to allow their child more time for sleep, and in particular allow them time to catch up with their sleep on non-school days. Waking them up early at the weekends for family activities may actually be damaging both their health and their educations. Other tips to help with this problem:

- Avoid caffeine in the afternoons and evenings.
- Avoid studying and using computers for at least an hour before bedtime.
- If a teenager has too much in his / her schedule, drop some of the less-important commitments.
- If a teenager has too much homework, parents could ask the school for the total amount to be reduced.
- Parents and schools can discuss starting the school day later. In the State of Minnesota, USA, some schools moved the starting time forward by 50 minutes, and soon noticed improved grades.

Green Line Oberstufe Klasse 10
ISBN: 978-3-12-560021-8

11 Mediation: Exchanging information

Liz, an exchange student from the UK, is staying at your house. Your friend Hannes has been working in his school to increase understanding about the problem of bullying and has written articles about it for the school magazine. Liz doesn't think bullying is a serious problem. Hannes wants to discuss this, but his English isn't very good.
Help to communicate between him and Liz. Choose your words carefully. Hannes has very strong opinions about this subject, so leave out anything you think is impolite.

Liz: I don't think bullying is really a problem. Well, it isn't at my school.

You: (1) ____________________

Hannes: Das ist unwahrscheinlich, denn in den meisten Ländern geben ca. 90% der befragten Schüler an, dass sie drangsaliert werden. Vielleicht merkst du einfach nicht, was du nicht merken willst.

You: (2) ____________________

____

Liz: I go to an all-girls school. I guess bullying is mainly a problem among boys.

You: (3) ____________________

Hannes: Das ist Unsinn. Untersuchungen zeigen, dass es Mobbing fast gleichermaßen unter Jungen wie auch Mädchen gibt.

You: (4) ____________________

____

Liz: Really? I've never seen girls fight with other girls at my school.

You: (5) ____________________

____

Hannes: Körperliche Übergriffe sind nicht die einzige Form von Mobbing. Es gibt verschiedene Arten: verbale Attacken, wie Menschen beschimpfen oder verspotten, aber auch soziale Ausgrenzung, also wenn man Menschen aus einer Gruppe ausschließt, und üble Nachrede.

You: (6) ____________________

____

____

Liz: OK, there's some of that at my school, it's true.

You: (7) ____________________

Hannes: Da bin ich mir ganz sicher. Und natürlich gibt es auch noch ‚cyber-bullying'. Das heißt, man benutzt das Internet oder schreibt SMS, um jemanden zu drangsalieren. Hast du schon mal jemanden eine gemeine SMS geschickt?

You: (8) ____________________

____

Green Line Oberstufe Klasse 10
ISBN: 978-3-12-560021-8

Liz: Well, perhaps once or twice. But don't you think it's just a temporary thing some kids go through? They grow out of it soon enough.

You: (9) ______________________________

____

____

Hannes: Wie kann man nur so naiv sein? Gibt es nicht schon genug grausame Menschen auf der Welt! Was meinst du, wie die angefangen haben? Jeder muss begreifen, dass Mobbing nicht normal ist – weder in der Schule, noch sonst irgendwo.

You: (10) ______________________________

____

____

Liz: But doesn't reporting bullying just make things worse for the person who is being bullied?

You: (11) ______________________________

____

Hannes: Nein, in Schulen, in denen Maßnahmen gegen Mobbing eingeleitet wurden, hat sich die Situation verbessert. Schulen brauchen eine Kultur, in der Mobbing nicht akzeptiert, sondern bestraft wird. Die Opfer müssen sich an die Lehrer wenden, denn sonst ändert sich nichts – weder für sie, noch für zukünftige Schüler der Schule.

You: (12) ______________________________

____

____

____

Liz: OK, OK, I get the message. There's no need to bully me!

You: (13) ______________________________

____

Green Line Oberstufe Klasse 10
ISBN: 978-3-12-560021-8

Topic 2 Multi-ethnic Britain

1 Listening: Latin Americans in London

Either:
Listen to the report about the Latin American community in the United Kingdom. Tick (✔) the correct endings to the sentences. Only one is correct.

1. Since 2001, the Latin American population has …
   a) increased four times in size. ☐
   b) decreased four times in size. ☐
   c) stayed the same. ☐

2. … Latin Americans live in the UK.
   a) Over 200,000 ☐
   b) Over 300,000 ☐
   c) Over 400,000 ☐

3. About as many Latin Americans live in London as …
   a) Australians. ☐
   b) Greeks. ☐
   c) Pakistanis. ☐

4. Most Latin Americans arrived in London during the …
   a) 1960s. ☐
   b) 1970s. ☐
   c) 1980s. ☐

5. They now come to the UK more than the USA because …
   a) they prefer England to any other country. ☐
   b) the terrorist attacks in the US mean it's too difficult to go to the US. ☐
   c) life is cheaper in the UK. ☐

6. The percentage of Latin Americans in the UK who can't speak English well is …
   a) about 30%. ☐
   b) about 50%. ☐
   c) about 70%. ☐

7. Two-thirds of the second generation have …
   a) had no problems integrating. ☐
   b) experienced racism. ☐
   c) enjoy living in the UK. ☐

8. In London, the biggest Latin American communities are in …
   a) Notting Hill. ☐
   b) Lambeth and Southwark. ☐
   c) Chelsea. ☐

Or:
Listen to the report. Put the following statements (A – H) into the same order in which the information occurs in the report (1 – 8).

____ A The majority of the second generation originate from Colombia.

____ B One-third of Latin Americans in the UK can't speak English.

____ C Two-thirds of the second generation have experienced racism and discrimination.

____ D The cultural influence of Latin Americans can be seen all over London.

____ E A large proportion of second-generation Latin Americans are on state benefits.

____ F Most Latin Americans in London come from Colombia, Ecuador and Brazil.

____ G In 2008, about 113,500 Latin Americans were living in London.

____ H More than 10% are paid less than the national minimum wage.

Green Line Oberstufe Klasse 10
ISBN: 978-3-12-560021-8

2 Listening: Multiculturalism in the UK

Either:
Listen to the radio interviews. Are these statements true or false?
Tick (✔) the right box..

	true	false
1. Liyu was born in the UK.		
2. His parents met while they were living in China.		
3. Liyu can speak both English and Cantonese.		
4. When he finishes his A-levels, he wants to become a vet.		
5. Liyu feels more British than Chinese.		
6. Maryam's parents left Iran to find work in the UK.		
7. Maryam thinks that the UK and Iran are very similar.		
8. Homosexuality is tolerated in Iran.		
9. Maryam eats both British and Iranian food.		
10. She speaks Farsi with her parents.		

Or:
Listen and answer the questions in not more than six words.

1. When did Liyu's parents move to the UK?

____

2. Which part of London do they live in?

____

3. What languages do they speak at home?'

____

4. What's Liyu's favourite festival?

____

5. What job does Maryam's father do?

____

6. Why did Maryam find life difficult when she came to the UK?

____

7. When does Maryam eat traditional Persian food?

____

Green Line Oberstufe Klasse 10
ISBN: 978-3-12-560021-8

3 Reading: Illegal immigrants

"Get in the lorry. Hurry up! Go now!" my mother said as she pushed me away from her.
I did exactly what she said and joined the others as they climbed into the lorry on the dark car park. A man gave me his hand and roughly pulled me inside. Handing me a plastic bag, he pointed to a space at the back.
I knew that the officials[1] at British ports had machines to detect[2] carbon dioxide emissions and that when we arrived I would put the bag over my head to hide the $CO2$ in my breath.

The lorry was on its way to the UK, and was transporting tractor tyres[3] from China to be sold to English farmers.
I hid myself inside a big tyre where no one could see me. I paused to look at my mum. I met her eyes and saw tears appear in them. She tried to smile, causing her face to screw up in a grimace[4]. The doors of the lorry were pulled closed by the driver and, although I didn't know it at the time, that was the last time I saw my mother.

The inside of the lorry was now completely black and it smelt strongly of rubber and something else I couldn't identify. I could hear the sounds of other people breathing.
I was rocked from side to side by the movement of the lorry. I don't know how, but I managed to go to sleep. The journey was very long. I'm not sure how many days exactly because there was no telling the difference between day and night. I felt the lorry stop and I heard people shouting. Quickly pulling the plastic bag over my head, I lay down inside a tractor tyre.
I heard the doors of the lorry being pulled open and officials telling everyone to come out of their hiding places. I heard a woman's voice above me. "There's another one hiding over here. It's a young boy. Come on darling; out you get." Taking the plastic bag off my head, I saw an Indian-looking woman in her fifties with kind eyes looking down at me. "Come on; climb up out of there." I did as I was told and joined the others next to the lorry. The woman who had discovered me then motioned for me to follow her. Walking across a car park, we arrived at a small windowless office and she indicated that I should sit down on a plastic chair.

Then she left and returned a short time later carrying a cup of tea, which she handed to me. "Mind yourself. It's hot. Just hang on a tick and another officer will come to interview you." A few moments later, a very tall black man entered the small office.
He sat down at the desk, took out a pen and started to write on a form he had brought with him.

"Where are you from?"
I looked at the immigration officer blankly[5]. His accent was very different to the ones I had heard in my English classes at school. He asked me again, this time speaking more slowly.
"Where – are – you – from?"
"Iraistan," I answered. "I'm a political refugee[6]. I have come to England to be safe from the fighting that is happening in my country."
The immigration officer looked surprised.
"What's your name?"
"Tomu", I replied.
"How old are you?" he asked me.
"16" I told him.
"Can you tell me more about why you tried to enter the UK illegally?"
I looked at him and, taking a deep breath, I prepared to tell him my story …

[1]**official** a person employed by the state, i.e. a police officer or a customs official;
[2]**to detect** to discover the existence of something;
[3]**tyre** the rubber part of the wheel;
[4]**to screw up in a grimace** to make an ugly expression with your face to show pain or unhappiness;
[5]**blankly** showing no feeling;
[6]**refugee** person who has been forced to leave their country or home

Green Line Oberstufe Klasse 10
ISBN: 978-3-12-560021-8

Either:
Read Tomu's story. Are these statements true, false or not in the text? Tick (✔) the right box.

	true	false	not in text
1. The lorry was going to the United Kingdom.			
2. Tomu will see his mother again.			
3. Tomu is alone in the lorry.			
4. The journey is very quick.			
5. Tomu is given a lot of food to eat.			
6. The female immigration officer is very kind.			
7. Tomu wants to stay in the UK permanently.			
8. Tomu finds it difficult to understand the second immigration officer's pronunciation.			
9. The second immigration officer was the son of immigrants to the UK.			
10. Tomu left Iraistan because life there was too dangerous.			

Or:
Read the text and finish the sentences in your own words.

1. The inside of the lorry was ______
2. The man handed Tomu a plastic bag because ______
3. Tomu hid himself ______
4. After giving Tomu a cup of tea, the female officer said ______
5. The immigration officer's accent ______
6. The protagonist is leaving Iraistan because ______

Analysis:
Analyse the text by answering the following questions.

1. What type of text is it? ______
2. Where might this type of text come from? ______
3. Who could the author be? ______
______
4. What is the author's intention? ______
______

Green Line Oberstufe Klasse 10
ISBN: 978-3-12-560021-8

4 Reading: British-born Chinese

(1) My parents are from China; my mum is from Chongqing and my dad is from a province called Anhui in East China, close to Shanghai. They grew up in those places. At the start of the Cultural Revolution they were about 18 years old and had just finished high school. Because of the change of politics, they were forced to go to the countryside to work as farmers. They didn't actually start university until they were probably in their late twenties – they went on to study engineering at Guangzhou University in the 1970s and 1980s. After graduating[1], and having taught for a few years, my father wanted to study for a higher qualification. He came over to do a PhD[2] at Oxford University, and my mum came over a few years later to be with my dad.

(2) Having studied English before he came to the UK, my father could actually speak to people, so it was easier for him to integrate into British society. I think it was more difficult for my mum, as she had no previous knowledge of English. However, my mum is much more open than my father – she does like to chat a lot and it helped her to learn English quickly. She just wants to communicate with everyone, whereas my dad, who does speak English really well, doesn't like speaking the language. In my opinion, I think it's very hard for anyone to move to a completely different society and learn a foreign language, no matter where they're from.

(3) I was born in Oxford in 1990. I've always lived in the UK, but we've moved houses a couple of times. While I remember growing up in Oxford, my memories of the place aren't that good. I went to nursery school in Oxford and then we moved to London because of my dad's job. I went to primary school in London – this is my first real memory.

(4) My mum has always been quite independent and not very traditionally Chinese. Whereas my father is very traditional and is more family-oriented. I guess I'm a mixture of both my parents' characteristics.

(5) I had an English babysitter while my parents worked, which was a great help in understanding British culture and society. I feel British probably because my identity was something that I never talked about. I was also born in the UK and I've lived here all my life, therefore, I'd say I'm British because it's easier. At home we speak both English and Mandarin.

(6) My parents have always raised me with a very strong work ethic[3], which I suppose is a traditional Chinese belief. When they were growing up they didn't have as many opportunities as I had. The Cultural Revolution prevented them from doing exactly what they wanted to do. That's the main reason they came to the UK – raising their children in a Western society would allow them to have more freedom. I'd also say that I'm quite modest[4], which is typical of Chinese people. They don't like to draw attention to themselves, which makes them great citizens. However, it means you can be quite invisible[5] and you perhaps don't have as much prominence[6], certainly compared to some of the other ethnic groups that are in the UK.

[1]**to graduate** to finish university; [2]**PhD** a doctorate;
[3]**work ethic** the principle that hard work is a good habit and should be rewarded;
[4]**modest** being quiet about your own abilities and achievements;
[5]**invisible** hidden, unable to be seen; [6]**prominence** being important and very noticeable

Green Line Oberstufe Klasse 10
ISBN: 978-3-12-560021-8

Either:
Read the text and match the interview questions below with paragraphs 1–6.
One of the questions doesn't fit any paragraph.

____ Do you share the same characteristics as your parents or are there differences?

____ What was your childhood like?

____ Have you experienced racism in the UK?

____ What areas of Chinese and British culture do you like?

____ What do you think life was like for your parents when they first moved to the UK?

____ When you were growing up, did you feel more British or more Chinese

____ Could you tell us about your origins?

Or:
Read the text. Are these statements true or false? Write down the lines of the text where the information can be found. Correct the false statements.

	true	false	line(s)
1. The parents worked as farmers before going to university.			
2. Both parents were able to speak English before coming to the UK.			
3. The mother is very shy.			
4. The writer thinks that it's difficult to learn a foreign language wherever you are from.			
5. The writer's earliest memory is going to a nursery school in Oxford.			
6. The author takes after both her parents.			
7. The author regards herself as being British.			
8. Their main reason for coming to the UK was to give their children a better future.			
9. The author shares some characteristics of Chinese people.			
10. The Chinese community in the UK doesn't like to attract attention.			

Analysis:
Analyse the text by answering the following questions.

1. How is this text different from the *Illegal immigrants* text in section 3?
2. What does the text tell you about the author?
3. What's the purpose of the text?

Green Line Oberstufe Klasse 10
ISBN: 978-3-12-560021-8

5 Understanding films: Leicester – a multi-ethnic city

Either:
Watch the film. Match the sentences below to the person who says them.
Write (H) for head teacher, (R) for reporter, or (P) for passers-by.

1. The Rushey Mead School is made up of 95% Asian and black students.	
2. Those students get a good deal.	
3. It would be boring if it were just a full-white community, but with the mixed-racing here, it's not.	
4. I've lived here for all my life and when I was younger I used to get picked on by white people, but now they don't bother me.	
5. The local council believes that the key for cities like this is to see diversity as being positive.	
6. The predicted population changes in places like Leicester and Birmingham reflect the changing face of British society and, ultimately, what it means to be British.	

Or:
Summarize the film clip in three sentences.

____

____

____

____

____

____

____

____

Analysis:
Analyse the film by answering the following questions.

1. What type of film is it?
2. Where is ist set?
3. Who are the people in the film?
4. What's the purpose of the film?
5. How is multiculturalism shown visually?

Green Line Oberstufe Klasse 10
ISBN: 978-3-12-560021-8

6 Writing: A letter to the editor

Write a letter to the editor of a magazine discussing the topic of the cartoon. Write about 150 words.

- Present the situation shown in the cartoon.
- Interpret the message the cartoonist wishes to convey.
- Do you think the message also applies to Germany? Explain why / why not.

" I say, *if they want to live in this country, they should follow our culture* . . . By the way, what do you want for dinner - *Mexican, Chinese or Italian* ? "

7 Writing: A report

Write a report discussing the information in the statistics. Write about 150 words.

- Present the situation shown in the statistics.
- Interpret the results of the statistics. What are the effects of this situation?
- Describe your impression of the situation in your country, but without quoting statistics.

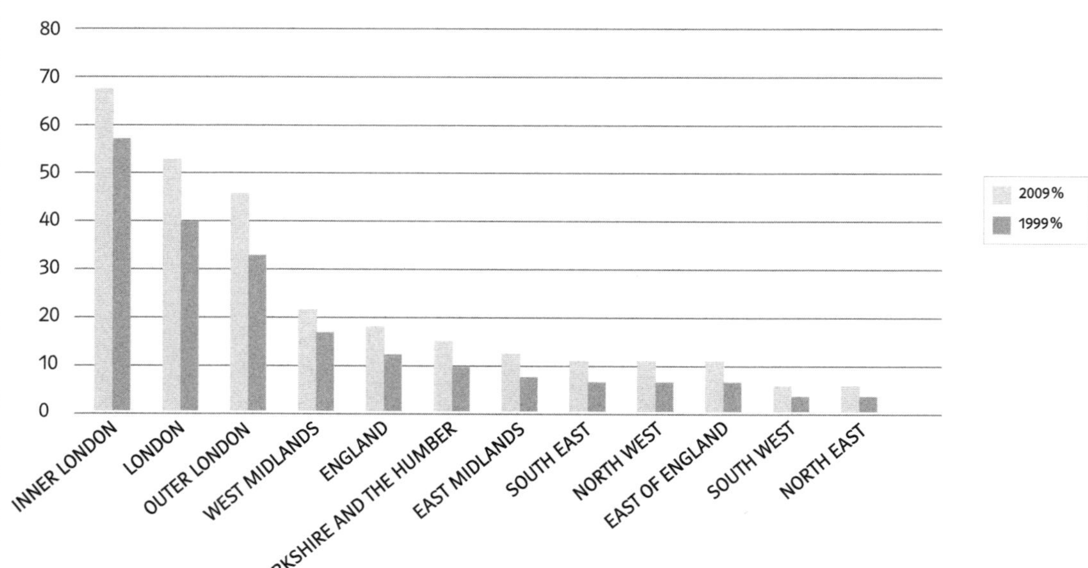

© Kings College

Green Line Oberstufe Klasse 10
ISBN: 978-3-12-560021-8

8 Speaking: Cultural tolerance

Part 1: Interview:

1. What can you see in the photo?
2. What has happened?
3. Why do you think this has happened?

Part 2: Individual long turn

Student A: *Give an example of cultural tolerance. Are there limits? Where do you stand on this issue?*

Student B: *Should German laws be changed to accommodate the different cultural traditions of minority cultures?*

Part 3: Discussion

Student A: *You are of the opinion that women should be banned from wearing the burqa in the UK. Find arguments for this point of view. Then discuss the topic with your partner.*

Student B: *You are of the opinion that people who live in multi-ethnic societies should tolerate and respect what other people wear. Find arguments for this point of view. Then discuss the topic with your partner.*

Picture 1

Picture 2

Green Line Oberstufe Klasse 10
ISBN: 978-3-12-560021-8

9 Speaking: Cultural heritage

Part 1: Interview:

1. What can you see in photo 1?
2. Why do you think the people in photo 1 are so happy? What do you think might have happened?
3. Describe the impression given by photo 2 when placed in contrast to photo 1.
4. Explain how the juxtaposition of the photos influences the way we interpret them.

Picture 1

Picture 2

Part 2: Individual long turn

Student A: *The two photos above are a 'study in contrasts'. Explain what this means.*

Student B: *What's the 'message' of the two photos above?*

Part 3: Role-play

Student A: *Choose one of the students in photo 1 and invent a possible biography. Have a conversation with your partner about your cultural background.*

Student B: *Choose one of the students in photo 1 and invent a possible biography. Have a conversation with your partner about your cultural background.*

Green Line Oberstufe Klasse 10
ISBN: 978-3-12-560021-8

10 Mediation: A summary

In your social studies class you are talking about the cultural changes which have been taking place in Europe. Summarize this article from a British newspaper about the cultural influence of the Arab world in the UK.
Write your summary in German. It should contain the information necessary to answer the following questions: English, you summarize the main arguments of the article for them in German.

1. How many Arabs live in the UK?
2. Which countries do they come from?
3. When did they start immigrating to the UK? Why?
4. How is Arab culture evident in London?
5. Where do many Arabs in London choose to live?

London: An Arabian love story

More than half a million Arabs now live in the UK, and most of them choose to live in London. The majority come from Egypt, Morocco, Palestine, Yemen, Lebanon, the Gulf States and Iraq.

Britain and the Arab world have been doing business for a very long time. In the middle of the 19th century, seamen from Yemen lived around the river Thames in London and there is still a large Yemini community today. The 1930s saw many Iraqis coming to live and work in London. This was followed by a large Egyptian migration in the 1940s and 1960s. The migrants who came to England were a mix of professional and unskilled workers. During the 1950s and 1960s, general Arab migration to Britain increased as the Arab world struggled to emerge from the era of colonialism.

With the money earned from oil, the migrants from the Gulf States set up businesses in London. More migrants arrived from Lebanon in the 70s, escaping the war in their country. The same is true for Iraqis who came to live in the UK in the 1980s and 1990s.

Arab culture can be seen all over London, which contributes to the multicultural flavour of the capital, and it appears not only in the form of Lebanese kebab shops, shisha bars and Moroccan restaurants, but also in clothing. The Emirates logo can be seen on a football shirt worn by thousands of fans. A North London football club signed a £100 million sponsorship deal with the Dubai airline in 2004.

The centre of London, including SW1, NW London, W2 and W1 - particularly around Edgeware Road – has many Arabs living there. The Borough of Westminster, one of the richest places to live in London, has the highest number of Arabic speakers. Knightsbridge is another example, with its nightclubs, banks, restaurants and of course Harrod's, which was owned for many years by the Egyptian Mohamed Al-Fayed and now belongs to an investment company from Quatar.leep at 2 a.m., and why it can then be so difficult for them to jump out of bed feeling lively at 7a.m.

Green Line Oberstufe Klasse 10
ISBN: 978-3-12-560021-8

11 Mediation: Chinese New Year

You and your brother are visiting London and you want to go and see the Chinese New Year celebrations. Your brother wants to ask a Chinese passer-by some questions, but he doesn't speak English as well as you do and he asks you to help him.

Brother: Wie feiert man das chinesische Neujahr und wann?

You: (1) ______________________________

Passer-by: In 2013, Chinese New Year takes place on 10th February. There is a huge festival with traditional dances in Trafalgar Square. There are also a lot of fireworks and music, and of course lots of things to eat!

You: (2) ______________________________

____

____

Brother: Welchem Tierzeichen wird denn das Jahr 2013 zugeordnet?

You: (3) ______________________________

Passer-by: It's the year of the snake. It means that nobody in your house will go hungry. It'll be a good year for doing business, but a bad year for moving house or getting married.

You: (4) ______________________________

____

____

Brother: Ich bin im Jahr des Affen geboren – welche Eigenschaften habe ich?

You: (5) ______________________________

____

Passer-by: Hmmm, well – we think monkeys are clever and talkative, but they get bored very easily. Does this sound like you?

You: (6) ______________________________

____

Brother: Haha! Ein bisschen. Können Sie mir mehr über das Neujahrsfest erzählen?

You: (7) ______________________________

____

Passer-by: All the family meet and eat a big dinner together. Children are given money in little red envelopes.

You: (8) ______________________________

____

Brother: Thank you very much. That was interesting.

Green Line Oberstufe Klasse 10
ISBN: 978-3-12-560021-8

Topic 3 The Blue Planet

1 Listening: Enough is enough!

Either:

Listen to six people expressing their opinion about a plan to build a new runway at Heathrow Airport in London. Match each speaker to one of the opinions below. The first one has been done for you.

Opinion	Speaker
a) The government aren't interested in the population who don't fly.	
b) I want to preserve the way of life I have always known.	
c) It would be very bad if London was left behind by neighbouring countries.	
d) There doesn't seem to be an end in sight to the continued expansion of the airport.	1
e) Airport expansion will bring far more benefits than problems.	
f) Noise pollution is the only reason why I might move out of the area.	

Or:

Listen to six people expressing their opinion about a plan to build a new runway at Heathrow Airport in London. Underline the correct answer to complete each sentence. The first one has been done for you.

1. According to Speaker 1, in the last 20 years noise pollution in the area has **<u>increased</u> / decreased / stayed the same**.
2. According to Speaker 1, governments usually support airport expansion for **environmental / economic / tourism** reasons.
3. Speaker 2 thinks that there will be **half / twice / three times** as many air passengers in the next 20 years.
4. Speaker 3 is worried about a time when there will be no more **oil / money / tourists**.
5. According to Speaker 4, most local people have to stay in the area despite possible dangers to their **children / homes / health**.
6. Speaker 5 says that in future, planes will make less **noise / pollution / money**.
7. According to Speaker 6, lots of **schools / houses / farms** would have to be destroyed in order to build the new runway.

Green Line Oberstufe Klasse 10
ISBN: 978-3-12-560021-8

2 Listening: Green shoppers

Either:
Listen to an extract from a radio programme about Green Consumerism. Number the following ideas according to the order in which they are talked about. The first one has been done for you.

a) Financial considerations ______

b) Short term v long term benefits. ______

c) Feeling guilty 1

d) Familiarity with products ______

e) Why it matters ______

f) Confusing advertising techniques ______

Or:
Listen to an extract from a radio programme about Green Consumerism.
Are these statements true or false? Tick (✔) the right box.

	true	false
1. The shopping habits of some consumers don't match their beliefs.		
2. Advertisers never give misleading information about the contents of their products.		
3. Most people are well-informed about the advantages of eco-friendly products.		
4. Conventional products are more frequently shown on television than eco-friendly products.		
5. Most people are more concerned about themselves than the environment when making shopping decisions.		
6. People are right to think that eco-friendly products are always more expensive.		
7. Buying eco-friendly products sends an important message to businesses.		

Green Line Oberstufe Klasse 10
ISBN: 978-3-12-560021-8

3 Reading: A poem

Not guilty

I want clean air, I want clean water
I want a safe world for my son or my daughter
But that's in the future, I still have time
You see, I am young and the fault is not mine

I didn't pollute this unbreathable air
I didn't make holes in the ozone layer
I don't want the ice caps to disappear
Can nobody stop it? Does nobody hear?

Did I build the factories that darken the sky?
I didn't, but perhaps I should watch what I buy
If their products are cheap, how much should I ask
About how they were made, who was given the task?

We want smartphones, cheap clothing and coffee to go
How were they all made, do we want to know?
We're young, we're not guilty, but we decide what we do
Will we allow this disaster to be our fault, too?

Either:
Complete this summary of the main ideas in the poem by choosing a word for each gap from the box. There are more words than you need. The first one (0) has been done for you.

angry • solution • disasters • environment • produced • behaviour • clothes • generations • happy • choices • responsible • world • damage • sold

Young people like the writer want to live in a clean, safe (0) world and they are not (1) ____________ for the damage that has been done to the (2) ____________ by (3) ____________ before their own. The writer is (4) ____________ that nobody seems to be doing anything to stop the environmental (5) ____________ that are happening. However, as she begins to ask herself questions about her own (6) ____________, she realises that she buys things which have probably been (7) ____________ in an environmentally-unfriendly way. In the end, she says that young people have important (8) ____________ to make. They must be careful not to become part of the problem.

Green Line Oberstufe Klasse 10
ISBN: 978-3-12-560021-8

Or:
Read the poem and answer the questions.

1. Does the writer have children?

____

2. Which three examples of environmental problems does the writer mention?

____

3. Which things might young people want that could be environmentally-unfriendly?

____

4. What problem does she see regarding cheap products?

____

5. What could young people do to remain "not guilty"?

____

Analysis:

1. *In which of the poem's lines do the following things happen?*
   a) The poet complains about what other people have done: lines ________ to ________
   b) The poet thinks about what she does: lines ________ to ________
   c) The poet warns young people that their own wishes might cause them to become guilty of damaging the environment: lines ________ to ________

2. *People accused of a crime are found "guilty" or "not guilty" in court. Do you think "Not guilty" is a good title for this poem? Say why or why not.*

____

____

____

____

____

3. *Look at the questions in the poem and say which questions have the following functions:*
   a) expressing frustration
   b) challenging the readers to think about their behaviour
   c) saying that the writer is not responsible for something

Green Line Oberstufe Klasse 10
ISBN: 978-3-12-560021-8

4 Reading: Amazon

In October 2007, adventurer Bruce Parry and his film crew went to South America to make a BBC television documentary series called 'Amazon'. He had previously presented a series called 'Tribe', about different tribes around the world. The new series would follow the course of the Amazon river. The following extracts are from the beginning of his book about the project.

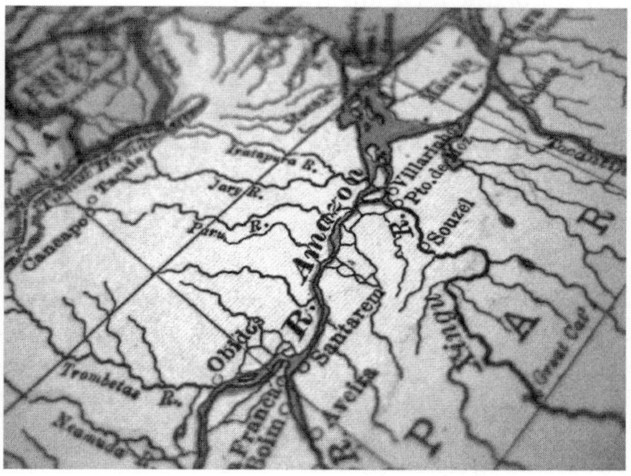

18 October, Heathrow

I'm in the departure lounge at Heathrow airport, setting off on a six-month trip to follow the Amazon from its source in the High Andes to the Atlantic coast in Brazil, where it releases a torrent of fresh water miles out into the ocean. I was on the road for three years making *Tribe*, and now I'm back travelling after a few months' break at home.

We've checked about fifty bags through customs, including a portable crane, countless cameras and a case full of medical equipment. On *Tribe* there was just a director, a cameraman and me – now we have a crew of six and a huge budget. There have been months of furious preparation. We will be filming in the most biodiverse region on earth, with some of the last uncontacted tribes, and we need all this equipment and expertise to do it as well as we can.

Amazon will be a new challenge for me in front of the camera. Unlike *Tribe*, I won't be staying in any one community for a long time to immerse[1] myself in their culture. Instead we'll be constantly journeying: this isn't an expedition in the sense that we'll march along the Amazon, but we will use the river as a rough route through the continent to tell the stories of the different people who depend on it.

Sometimes I will live with Amazonian tribes, but we plan to add more context than on *Tribe*, by showing the threats[2] to the tribes and their environment. I will spend time with the farmers, ranchers and gold miners of the Amazon, and share their culture in the same way as with the tribes we visit. We want to try to understand all sides of the story and to show it as objectively as possible.

The stories within the Amazon are complex and important, those of human lives affected by big-headline issues: the cocaine trade, logging[3] and slavery. They're stories important to the people and tribes of the Amazon; to Peru and to the rest of the world too, which is in itself a contentious[4] issue.

It's an exciting and intimidating[5] challenge, and it will begin after an eighteen hour flight to Peru – I'm sure Heathrow departure lounge will soon seem a million miles away.

26 October, Mismi

We have started. We're at the source, on a mountain called the Nevado Mismi, and filming has finally begun. Up here the landscape seems barren[6], almost lunar[7] at times – a vista[8] of parched[9] brown and dusty grey and a bright blue sky.

Green Line Oberstufe Klasse 10
ISBN: 978-3-12-560021-8

We walked here over a dry stony ground where wind builds the dust up and piles it around your boots, so you trek through it like snow. Most of the crew have been chewing coca leaves – the local remedy[10] for altitude[11] sickness, you wrap it up with charcoal, which acts as a catalyst to release the cocaine, to help your body deal with the reduced oxygen absorption at altitude. Inca culture has used coca leaf like this since ancient times and as the source itself is just under 5,200 metres, it's at a pretty extreme altitude. Everyone's suffering from nausea[12], headaches and an inability to sleep – you wake up gasping, unable to get enough oxygen. So I'm up for taking anything that can help.

The source itself is inspiring. The water literally pours out of a cliff face – spurts[13] of the cold crystal liquid gush[14] out of the rock. There's something elemental, mysterious and exciting about the place: this spring of water is the start of the world's biggest river.

[1]**to immerse yourself in something** to be completely involved;
[2]**a threat** an idea that something bad will happen; [3]**logging** cutting down trees;
[4]**contentious** describes something that people have strong opinions about;
[5]**intimidating** describes something that makes you feel nervous;
[6]**barren** empty, nothing grows there; [7]**lunar** like the moon;
[8]**a vista** a view; [9]**parched** very dry, thirsty;
[10]**a remedy** something you take to cure an illness;
[11]**altitude** height above sea level; [12]**nausea** feeling sick;
[13]**a spurt** a sudden, fast action; [14]**to gush** to pour very fast

Either:
Complete the grid with information given in the text about the three differences between the two television series, Tribe and Amazon.

Tribe	Amazon

Green Line Oberstufe Klasse 10
ISBN: 978-3-12-560021-8

Or:
Are these statements true, false or not in the text? Tick (✔) the right box.

	true	false	not in the text
1. Bruce Parry had a three-year break after making *Tribe*.			
2. They will be filming in a place which has more plants and animals than any other place in the world.			
3. They will stay on the river Amazon at all times during the filming of the documentary.			
4. In the documentary film Bruce Perry and his team want to examine the lives of different groups of people who depend on the river.			
5. Bruce Parry will live in the homes of Amazonian farmers, ranchers and miners.			
6. The documentary will also examine the various threats to the Amazonian tribes.			
7. Bruce Parry is excited and nervous at the same time.			
8. All of the crew feel sick on the first day of filming.			
9. Bruce Parry doesn't like the idea of chewing coca leaves.			

Analysis:

1. *State the main purpose of the text.*

2. *Analyse how the reader's interest in the text is influenced by its content and structure.*

3. *Illustrate the author's use of descriptive language to contrast the landscape of Nevado Mismo with the source of the river itself.*

Green Line Oberstufe Klasse 10
ISBN: 978-3-12-560021-8

5 Understanding films: Deforestation and global warming

Either:
Watch the film and then do the following tasks.

1. *Give two reasons why forests are cleared.*

2. *Give three ways in which wood from the trees is used.*

3. *How much longer might rainforests have to survive?*

4. *What is the predicted temperature rise by the end of the 21st century?*

5. *"Tropical rainforests are the lungs of the earth" is a quote from the beginning of the film. Explain what you think the presenter means by this.*

Or:
Write a short summary (about 60 words) of the film extract describing some of the causes and effects of global warming. Use the following prompts to help you with your summary.

Carbon-dioxide	→	The greenhouse effect
Sunbeams	→	Greenhouse gases
Human activity	→	More greenhouse gases
Global warming	→	Ice melts
Sea levels rise	→	Coastal regions flood
Salt content decreases	→	Species die out

Analysis:

1. *There are images in the film of rainforest being cleared, ice caps melting and water levels rising. What effect do these images have on the viewer?*

2. *Describe the effect the music has on the viewer.*

Green Line Oberstufe Klasse 10
ISBN: 978-3-12-560021-8

6 Writing: A letter to the editor

After seeing this cartoon in a newspaper, you decide to write a letter to the editor.

In your letter, you …

- briefly explain the expression "to bury your head in the sand".
- describe how the cartoonist has used irony to draw our attention to a serious issue.
- outline some ways in which many of us bury our heads in the sand over climate change, and some of the possible consequences of behaving in this way.

7 Writing: A speech

The Toad Transporter

A young girl walked carefully along the path to avoid stepping on the tiny toads that were crossing it and struggling on through long grass to start their long journey across a busy motorway to a lake on the other side. Impossible, she thought, but some toads must reach the lake. Enough to produce another generation of toads. Then she noticed that the old man ahead of her was picking up young toads and putting them into a plastic bag.
"Hello. What will you do with them?" she asked.
"There's a bridge about a mile from here. I carry them across it and take them to the lake," he explained.
"But you can only save a few. What difference does it make?"
The old man opened the bag and showed her the young toads inside.
"Well, it certainly makes a difference to them."

Your teacher has asked you to give a short speech to your class about what we can do to stop the environmental problems we are facing from getting any worse. You decide to use the story of "The Toad Transporter" as your starting point.

To prepare:

- Analyse the difference between the young girl's attitude and that of the old man.
- Explain the use of the toad as a metaphor.

Now write a short speech (about 100 words) discussing the importance of the old man's attitude with reference to the wider environmental issues we are facing in the world.

Green Line Oberstufe Klasse 10
ISBN: 978-3-12-560021-8

8 Speaking: The environment

Part 1: Interview:

1. Describe how important the natural environment is to you in your daily life.
2. Are you environmentally friendly? What do you do to show it?
3. What do you think future generations will think of the way we treated the environment?

Part 2: Individual long turn

Talk about one of the cartoons below. Describe some of the factors that have led to the environmental situation depicted in your cartoon. Say which of these factors you consider to be the most serious and explain why.

Cartoon 1

Cartoon 2

Part 3: Discussion

Student A: *You are of the opinion that it is essential that we all recycle as much of our rubbish as possible. Look at these arguments and find more arguments to support your view. Then discuss them with your partner.*

Possible arguments:
- *Saving of energy, water and oil*
- *Reduction of landfill sites*
- *Protection of natural resources*

Student B: *You are of the opinion that recycling creates problems. Look at these arguments and find more arguments to support your view. Then discuss them with your partner.*

Possible arguments:
- *Transportation – costs and pollution*
- *Glass needs washing – energy and water*
- *Plastic cheap to produce – more expensive to recycle*

Green Line Oberstufe Klasse 10
ISBN: 978-3-12-560021-8

9 Speaking: Energy and tourism

Part 1: Interview:

1. What kind of energy do you use?
2. Describe the environmental problems which concern you the most.
3. If you had the money, explain what kinds of energy you would invest in and why.

Part 2: Individual long turn

Student A: *Talk about your picture and about how we use energy in our homes.*

Student B: *Talk about your picture and about alternative energy sources we could use.*

Picture 1

Picture 2

Part 3: Discussion

Student A: *You are of the opinion that tourism causes many of the environmental problems we have in the world today. Look at these arguments and find more arguments to support this opinion. Then discuss them with your partner.*

Possible arguments:
- *Air travel*
- *Building of tourist facilities*
- *Crowds in places of natural beauty*

Student B: *You are of the opinion that the money and publicity generated by tourism can have a positive effect on the environment. Look at these arguments and find more arguments to support this opinion. Then discuss them with your partner.*

Possible arguments:
- *Tourism increases the public's awareness of environmental problems*
- *Tourist attractions such as national parks and historic buildings are economic assets*
- *The money generated by tourism supports natural habitats and animal protection services*

Green Line Oberstufe Klasse 10
ISBN: 978-3-12-560021-8

10 Mediation: A leaflet

You and a friend are doing a project called "Practical ways to help the planet". You have found an interesting leaflet on this subject. Your friend doesn't speak much English, so you'll have to explain the main ideas in German.
Summarize the texts, don't translate everything word for word!

1 TURN OFF COMPUTERS AT NIGHT
You can save energy and money by turning off your computer instead of leaving it in sleep mode. If you don't want to wait for your computer to start up, set it to turn on automatically a few minutes before you know you'll need to use it.

2 USE BOTH SIDES OF THE PAPER
We throw away millions of tons of paper every year. For a quick-and-easy way to reduce this waste, set your printer's default option to print both sides of a page. And when you're finished with your printouts, don't forget to take them to the recycling bin.

3 GO VEGETARIAN ONCE A WEEK
One less meat-based meal a week helps the planet and your diet. For example, it requires 2,500 gallons of water to produce one pound of beef. You will also save some trees. Did you know that approximately 17 square metres of forest have been destroyed for each hamburger made from animals raised on rainforest land?

4 RETHINK BOTTLED WATER
Nearly 90% of plastic water bottles are not recycled and they take thousands of years to decompose. Buy a reusable container and fill it with tap water – it will save you money and is a great choice for the environment.

5 BAN BATHTIME!
Have a no-bath week, and take showers instead. Baths require almost twice as much water. Not only will you reduce water consumption, but the energy needed to heat the water.

6 SECOND-HAND DOESN'T MEAN SECOND-BEST
Consider buying items from a second-hand store. Toys, bicycles, roller blades, and other age and size-specific items are quickly outgrown. Second-hand stores often sell these items in excellent condition since they are used for such a short period of time, and will generally buy them back when you no longer need them.

7 TURN OFF LIGHTS
Always turn off lights when you leave a room. You'll save a surprising amount of energy. In a hot climate it also saves cooling costs, as lights contribute heat to a room.

8 IT'S A WRAP!
Next time you give someone a present, make it extra special by creating your own environmentally-friendly wrapping paper. You can reuse gift bags, bows and event paper, but you can also make something unique by using old maps, cloth or even newspapers.

Green Line Oberstufe Klasse 10
ISBN: 978-3-12-560021-8

11 Mediation: Voluntary service

You have an American friend, Anna, staying at your house. Your parents' friend, Tom, is visiting. Tom works for an organisation which recruits volunteers to work on environmental projects in developing countries. Anna is very interested in volunteering and wants to find out more, but her German isn't very good.
Translate back and forth between Anna and Tom.

Anna: Where could I work? Which countries need volunteers?

Du: (1) …

Tom: Oh, viele Länder. Zum Beispiel beginnt bald ein neues und sehr wichtiges Projekt in Costa Rica.

Du: (2) …

Anna: I like the idea of Costa Rica. What's the project there?

Du: (3) …

Tom: Hm, es handelt sich um ein Tierschutzprojekt in einer Rettungsstation für Tiere im Süden des Landes. Dort wollen wir kranken Tieren helfen, um sie dann wieder in die Freiheit entlassen zu können. Die Freiwilligen vor Ort suchen nach verletzten Tieren, also solchen die beispielsweise von einem Auto angefahren wurden. Wenn sie wieder gesund sind, werden sie zurück in ihr Revier gebracht.

Du: (4) …

Anna: What would my job be?

Du: (5) …

Tom: Deine Aufgabe wäre es, dich um die Tiere zu kümmern bis sie wieder ausgesetzt werden können. Du würdest sie füttern, Daten sammeln, Vorträge vor Schulkindern halten und ihnen erklären, wie wichtig die Tier- und Pflanzenwelt ist. Aufklärung ist der wichtigste Teil des Jobs. Im Radio läuft sogar jede Woche eine Aufklärungskampagne für die du mit zuständig wärst – du würdest mit den Einheimischen über ihre Probleme sprechen.

Du: (6) …

Anna: It sounds great. I'd love to get involved. What should I do next?

Du: (7) …

Tom: Wir bieten in diesem Sommer einige Vorbereitungswochenenden an. Du kannst gern daran teilnehmen, um mehr über das Projekt zu erfahren und Gleichgesinnte kennenzulernen. Weißt du was, gib mir doch einfach deine E-Mailadresse, dann kann ich dir noch ein paar Informationen und den Bewerbungsbogen schicken.

Du: (8) …

Anna: Brilliant. Thanks.

Green Line Oberstufe Klasse 10
ISBN: 978-3-12-560021-8

Topic 4 South Africa

1 Listening: Visiting Robben Island

Either:
Lisa and her mother are on holiday in Cape Town, South Africa. Listen to their conversation. Are these statements true or false? Tick (✔) the right box.

	true	false
1. Mandela made Robben Island famous.		
2. Mandela was a prisoner on Robben Island all his life.		
3. Mandela never liked to talk to other prisoners about human rights.		
4. Mandela treated even his enemies with respect.		
5. Mandela helped other prisoners to get a good education.		
6. Mandela was kept in his cell all day long.		
7. Joseph Fiennes played a minor role in Goodbye Bafana, a film about Mandela.		
8. Mandela was a leader, even while he was in prison.		

Or:
Listen and complete the sentences about Lisa's visit to Cape Town.

1. Lisa travelled to Cape Town with ______
2. Lisa prepared for her visit by ______
3. Lisa had already watched a film about ______
4. Lisa was impressed by ______
5. Lisa looked forward to ______
6. For her trip on the boat, Lisa's mother asked her to take ______

Green Line Oberstufe Klasse 10
ISBN: 978-3-12-560021-8

2 Listening: The history of Robben Island

Either:
Listen and tick (✔) the correct answer. More than one can be correct

1. Who is one of the tour guides?
   a) a woman ☐
   b) an ex-prisoner ☐
   c) a 16-year-old boy ☐

2. Who wants to find out more about the island?
   a) politicians ☐
   b) tourists ☐
   c) teachers ☐

3. What has the old prison been converted into?
   a) a holiday camp ☐
   b) a hotel ☐
   c) a museum ☐

4. What do the tour guides talk about?
   a) tourism ☐
   b) the history of the island ☐
   c) the history of slavery ☐

Or:
Here are six sentences about Robben Island. Listen to the information and put the sentences into the correct historical order from past to present (1 – 6). The first one has been done for you.

A Robben Island was a prison for slaves who had tried to run away. ______

B Robben Island was a hospital for people with leprosy. ______

C Robben Island prison was converted into a human rights museum. ______

D Robben Island was a source of fresh food for European sailors. ______

E Robben Island was a prison for people who protested against Apartheid. ______

F Robben Island was an army base. ______

Green Line Oberstufe Klasse 10
ISBN: 978-3-12-560021-8

3 Reading: Storytelling in Africa

In South Africa, as in many other African countries, many people prefer listening to stories to reading books. As a result there are few bookshops outside the big cities, and people often don't know about local authors. But does this mean there's no literature in Africa? Of course not! There are plenty of African stories that are simply not written down. Africa has a rich oral tradition and the stories are in the minds of people who keep on telling them. Although many people now also record their stories, they are still better when performed live. That is why famous South African artists, such as Gcina Mhlope, travel around the country telling stories in schools and at festivals. This way the tradition of storytelling isn't lost. A story that is part of a live show always has parts where the audience can help the storyteller by shouting, clapping or singing along. Here's an example of a very short story that follows the oral traditions of the past.

Why the hyena laughs at night

One day Mr. Hyena was sitting under a tree. Nothing much was happening. He was hot and bored. Suddenly he saw a mouse running along. [Audience (1): clap, clap clap]. The mouse was small and brown.
"Hm, if I frighten the little mouse, I'll have a good laugh," Mr. Hyena thought to himself and smiled. "It looks very sweet and I'll play a clever trick."
The mouse came nearer [Audience (2): clap, clap clap]. When the mouse was really close, the hyena stood up. He shook his whole body like a dog. All this time he kept his eyes on the mouse. Finally he called the mouse over, using a sweet and friendly voice.
"Hey mouse, come here. I want to show you a strange new animal. I have it here in my tree. It looks like a tree crocodile."
The mouse was very curious. He loved to discover new things and so he quickly ran to the tree [Audience (3): clap, clap clap].
"A tree crocodile? How big is a tree crocodile?" the mouse asked.
"Smaller than you," said Mr. Hyena. "Come closer and have a look. Don't be afraid."
The mouse carefully came closer [Audience (4): clap, clap clap].
"It's right here in the tree with the red flowers. The little crocodile was green this morning, but look! Now it's half green, half brown," Mr. Hyena said.
"You have a crocodile that's half green, half brown? Really?" The mouse came even closer and carefully looked into the tree. There he saw a small green-brown animal with large eyes and a long tail. When the animal saw the mouse looking, it turned its eyes this way and that. Then it slowly moved away, trying to hide behind a big red flower higher up in the tree. As soon as the animal's tail was near the red flower, something strange happened. The tail started to change colour. It slowly turned red. The mouse jumped back quickly [Audience (5): one clap]. From a safe distance he continued to look at the changing colours with big, surprised eyes.
"It's magic," Mr. Hyena whispered, moving closer to the mouse. "This isn't a crocodile, but a bad spirit. Now it will turn you into a rat."
"Help", shouted the mouse and turned white with fear. He jumped down and ran away as quickly as his legs could carry him [Audience (6): clap, clap clap]. All that was left was the sand on the road. The hyena laughed a nasty laugh [audience: ha, ha, ha]. He thought it was funny that the mouse had never seen a chameleon before. Once again Mr. Hyena laughed with a loud laugh [Audience: ha, ha, ha].
"The mouse thought it was a bad thing," Mr. Hyena shouted. Then he laughed and laughed. He couldn't stop laughing for a very long time [Audience: ha, ha, ha, ha, ha, ha].

Hyenas still tell the story of the mouse who ran away from a chameleon. They think it's a very funny story. At the end of the story they laugh and laugh late into the night. Sometimes when you're in bed you can still hear them laughing. Isn't that right?

Green Line Oberstufe Klasse 10
ISBN: 978-3-12-560021-8

Either:
During a storytelling performance the clapping is used to add to the excitement and help give meaning to the story. Look at each time the audience claps and decide how the audience should clap. For example, should it be fast, slow, loud or soft? Write your answer like this:

1. fast claps (to sound like a running mouse)
2. ______
3. ______
4. ______
5. ______
6. ______

Or:
It is unusual for the audience of a folk tale to be on the side of the bad character. But here the audience laughs with the hyena. Complete these sentences to describe what effect this has on you.

1. When the audience laughs with the hyena I feel ______
2. I think the storyteller wants the audience to laugh, because ______
3. The laughter adds to the meaning of the story, because ______
4. If I told the story I would ______

Analysis:
Discuss the moral of the story. What does the story say about the power of knowledge? And what does it show about the way this power can be used?

Green Line Oberstufe Klasse 10
ISBN: 978-3-12-560021-8

4 Reading: Mama Africa

Miriam Makeba was the first South African singer to make African music popular all over the world. As early as 1957 her songs were at the top of the charts. Everyone loved the way her music mixed modern jazz with older African music in a completely new way. Some of her most famous hits were a Zulu wedding song, known as the Click Song, Pata Pata and Maleika. In 1959 Miriam Makeba was invited by Harry Belafonte to sing in the USA. This was her chance to become a famous singer and she grabbed it with both hands.

Miriam Makeba quickly became an international star while she lived in the USA. In this time she often used interviews to speak about the need for human rights in South Africa. Just over a year later, however, she found out the high price she would have to pay for her words. In 1960 Miriam Makeba's mother suddenly became very ill. When Miriam Makeba wanted to return to South Africa to see her, she was told that her South African passport was no longer valid. It had been cancelled by the Apartheid government. Without a passport Miriam Makeba was in exile. She could no longer return home.
"I always wanted to leave home. I never knew they were going to stop me from coming back. Maybe, if I had known I wouldn't be able to see my mother again, I would never have left," she said in an interview in 2004. In the same interview she tried to explain how hard it was for her to accept that because she stood up for human rights, her passport had been taken away. "Nobody will know the pain of exile until you are in exile.
It means you are always with people, but you are not one of them. That's when it hurts."
Her feelings didn't change, even when she was given passports by at least five other countries. In her heart South Africa would always be her home.

Many people recognized that Miriam Makeba was an excellent human rights activist. That is how she came to represent Guinea at the United Nations and won the Dag Hammarskjöld Peace Prize in 1986.
In 2001 she was also given the Otto Hahn Peace Medal in Berlin.

Being in exile did not stop Miriam Makeba from singing. As a singer she had a brilliant international career. She recorded with Harry Belafonte and performed with Paul Simon on the Graceland Tour. In 1974 she sang at the famous 'Rumble in the Jungle' boxing match between Muhammad Ali and George Foreman in Zaire. For many fans she became the face of African music and soon her nickname was Mama Africa. This made her feel proud. She also performed in at least 15 films and much later she sang at the Free Nelson Mandela Concert in 1988. All her life she worked to end Apartheid, so that she could go home.

When Mandela was released from prison in 1990, it was no surprise that he asked Miriam Makeba to come back to South Africa. After thirty-one years her passport was returned and she was finally able to re-enter the country of her birth. Soon after her arrival she gave a concert in Johannesburg and sang many of her favourite songs, which until then the people of South Africa had never heard live. The concert hall was packed and everybody had a great time. The crowd laughed and cheered when she sang songs like the Click Song, Welele and Aluta Continua. Many people knew the words and sang along. Her last song at the concert was Mama. As soon as she started singing the first few words, the crowd was very quiet and stood still to show respect. They knew it was the song Miriam Makeba had written when she hadn't been allowed to come and say goodbye to her mother so many years before.

Green Line Oberstufe Klasse 10
ISBN: 978-3-12-560021-8

Either:
Read the text about Miriam Makeba and outline the main events in her life …

1. *as a performing artist.*

____

____

____

____

2. *as a human rights activist.*

____

____

____

____

____

Or:
Is the following information true, false, or not in the text?

	true	false	not in the text
1. Miriam Makeba was born before 1957.			
2. Modern jazz is an important part of Miriam Makeba's music.			
3. Miriam Makeba left South Africa to fight the Apartheid government.			
4. Miriam Makeba acted in films.			
5. Miriam Makeba married Harry Belafonte.			
6. Nelson Mandela is a fan of Makeba's music.			
7. In the end Miriam Makeba got back her South African passport.			

Analysis:
How does the author of the article use the life of Miriam Makeba to illustrate that the Apartheid system wasn't good for black South Africans?

____

____

____

____

____

Green Line Oberstufe Klasse 10
ISBN: 978-3-12-560021-8

5 Understanding films: Cape Town, South Africa

a) *Watch the film and then complete these sentences.*

1. ______________________________ is South Africa's most famous landmark.
2. ______________________________ were the first Europeans to arrive there.
3. ______________________________ was the first to travel around the Cape and on to India.
4. ______________________________ were the first to build a castle in the Cape.
5. ______________________________ was South Africa's first fruit and vegetable patch.

b) *Here are four stills from the beginning of the film. Comment on the way the cinematic point of view is changing all the time. What is the effect of this camera technique on the viewer?*

Green Line Oberstufe Klasse 10
ISBN: 978-3-12-560021-8

6 Writing: Poverty in South Africa

A post on an Internet forum:

Poverty hits SA children, February 26, 2010, Times Live:

A new OECD working paper on poverty and income inequality in South Africa has found that more than half of all South Africans (54%) are poor, but among children below 10, as many as two out of three are poor. These high values are based on the national poverty line of 515 Rand a month, or about US$4 a day, which is used for national policy making. "There is little hope that the children will ever escape the poverty cycle," an OECD spokesperson said.

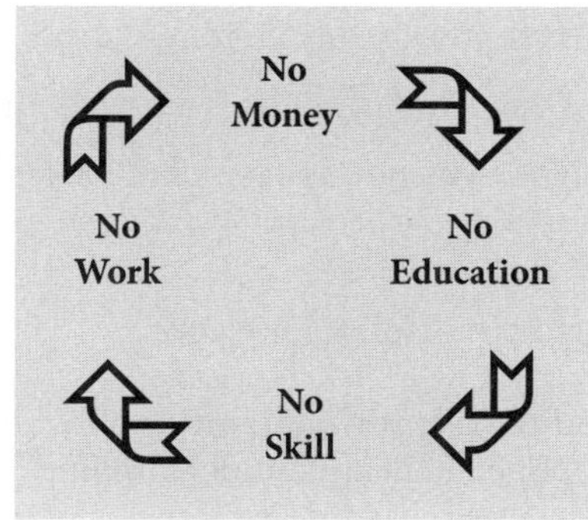

Do you agree that there is little hope for South Africa's poor children? After reading the above news report on the Internet you decide to post a comment (about 150 words) on the Times Live opinion page. Write down what you would like to say.

7 Writing: The breadline[1]

What does the woman think? Write a short narrative (about 200 words) to give a voice to her thoughts.

Published in the Independent Newspaper on 15. November, 2007

[1]**breadline** the lowest level of income on which it is possible to live

Green Line Oberstufe Klasse 10
ISBN: 978-3-12-560021-8

8 Speaking: Piercings

Part 1: Interview:

1. Have you got any piercings?
2. If yes, what was it like to have them done?
3. If no, why not? Can you imagine going for piercings in the future? Why? / Why not?

Part 2: Individual long turn

Traditionally the Zulu people of South Africa believed that by using ear plugs the mind is opened to deeper understanding.

Student A: *Look at the two images and discuss their similarities. Why you think these kinds of piercings are popular among some young people in Europe today?*

Student B: *Look at the two images and discuss their differences. Why you think these kinds of piercings are popular among some young people in Europe today?*

Picture 1

Picture 2

Part 3: Role-play

You want to get a tongue piercing at the weekend and you tell your parents about it. They're shocked and don't like the idea. Act out the situation with a partner in the role of one of your parents. Decide for yourselves how the discussion develops and what happens in the end.

Here are some expressions you might find helpful:

You must be out of your mind! • You always say that! • Look at it from my/our point of view • Anyway, … • You know, … • If you ask me, …, • To tell you the truth, … • Calm down! • I wish for once you would just …! • I/We think you are being … • Are you really sure about …? • Have you thought about …?

Green Line Oberstufe Klasse 10
ISBN: 978-3-12-560021-8

9 Speaking: An unusual house

Part 1: Interview:

Possible interview questions for the teacher

1. What's the most unusual house you have ever seen?
2. Have you ever dreamt of building your own house?
3. If yes, what would it look like? If no, why not?

Part 2: Individual long turn

In South Africa many people design and build their own houses. The structure of the house is often part of the way they express their individual style.

The photos below show two unusual houses in South Africa. Decide which one you would like to talk about. Then describe the house. Make sure you point out what makes it unusual. Who do you think lives in it? In conclusion give your personal opinion about the house and explain which features you like best / like the least.

Photo 1

The Shoe House in South Africa.

Photo 2

A house built from hand-made clay bricks (adobe) and painted in the traditional Ndebele style.

Part 3: Role-play

You're a travel writer and you visit the shoe house because it's on the list of the ten most unusual houses in the world. Now you want to interview the owner, Ron Van Zyl. Act out the interview with a partner. This table may help you:

travel writer	Ron van Zyl
when?	1990
why?	for wife
how?	Art gallery and coffee shop
visitors?	Yes / No, because ....

Green Line Oberstufe Klasse 10
ISBN: 978-3-12-560021-8

10 Mediation: The big prize!

South Africa is not only known for its beautiful landscapes and scenery, but unfortunately also for its poverty and high crime rate. To improve the country's reputation, South Africa's tourist board has launched an international competition. A woman from Germany is among the winners of a trip to South Africa. While she's there she keeps a blog. The manager of the South African Tourist Board is interested in the woman's impressions of the country, but doesn't know any German.
You're doing an internship at the Tourist Board. Help the manager to understand the woman's blog.

27.11.2012
Frankfurt Flughafen - 16:30 Uhr
Vor 3 Monaten bekam ich einen Anruf mit der unglaublichen Nachricht: ich habe eine Reise nach Südafrika gewonnen! Und jetzt ist es soweit. Ich sitze auf dem Frankfurter Flughafen und warte auf den Rest der Reisegruppe und den Check-In. Wie die Reise wohl wird?
(1) The writer …

28.11.2012
Ein langer Flug liegt hinter uns. Ich muss sagen, South African Airways ist sehr gut - sehr nette und aufmerksame Crew, das Essen einwandfrei. Erste Station heute ist Johannesburg mit Besuch in Soweto. Morgen geht's weiter nach Port Elizabeth.
(2) The trip to …

29.11.2012
Am Flughafen in Port Elizabeth wurden wir pünktlich abgeholt und erreichten nach etwa 90 Minuten die Zufahrt zum Amakhala Game Reserve, wo uns die Ranger bereits erwarteten. Unser Gepäck wurde in Jeeps umgeladen und dann ging es Richtung Hills Nek Lodge - unsere Unterkunft für die nächsten Tage. Schon auf dieser 20-minütigen Fahrt zur Lodge konnten wir uns einen ersten Eindruck von der grandiosen Landschaft machen. Auch begrüßten uns der erste Elefant an einem Wasserloch, Zebras am Wegesrand, und Antilopen in der Ferne.
(3) They were picked up at …

2.12.2012
Zwei unglaubliche Safaritage haben wir nun schon erlebt. Um 06:00 Uhr geht es immer los und David, der Ranger, bringt uns auf die Piste. Er ist immer freundlich und hilfsbereit. Mit viel Ruhe und Zeit können wir immer die Tiere beobachten und unsere Kameras klicken um die Wette.
(4) …

In der Ferne konnten wir heute eine Löwenfamilie erspähen und David versuchte sofort uns näher ran zu bringen. Mit etwas Geduld, Suche und viel Gespür klappte es auch! Wir kamen ganz dicht ran. Es war eine Löwenmutter mit fünf Halbwüchsigen. So wunderschöne und elegante Tiere, traumhaft gezeichnet, mit unglaublicher Eleganz und Kraft! Ich hätte sie stundenlang beobachten können!
(5) …

3.12.2012
Heute vormittag waren wir in Port Elisabeth auf dem Craft Market. Trotz der Menschenmenge habe ich mich eigentlich ganz sicher gefühlt. Ich liebe die Perlenarbeit[1], die die Leute hier machen. Ich habe gleich zehn Schlüsselanhänger aus Perlen[2] gekauft. Das sind phantastische Mitbringsel. Es ist gut etwas von dem Alltag der Menschen im Land zu sehen. In der Lodge begrüßte uns am frühen Abend Chantal mit ihrer freundlichen und herzlichen Art … und einem wiederum gigantischen Essen. Die guten Dinge nehmen einfach kein Ende.
(6) …

[1]**Perlenarbeit** beadwork; [2]**Perlen** beads

Green Line Oberstufe Klasse 10
ISBN: 978-3-12-560021-8

11 Mediation: A conversation

While you're doing an internship with the South African Tourist Board, you're invited to take part in an adventure trip geared towards young people. During the trip you're asked to keep a diary to note down your impressions. After the tour you take your German notes to the office and talk them through with Tim, one of your colleagues there.

Tims Fragen	Deine Notizen zu diesem Thema	Was sagst du zu Tim auf Englisch?
Which parts of the tour did you like best?	Elefantenreiten - auch wenn es alte Zirkustiere waren. Größe der Tiere sehr beeindruckend. Sollte auch Elefantensafari machen können!	(1)
Were there any activities you found boring?	Programm sehr abwechslungsreich. Zeit verging wie im Flug.	(2)
Would you like to comment on the accommodation?	Zeltlager cool, Holzboden im Zelt und Insektenschutz gute Idee, Schrank mit Schloss ganz wichtig. 4 Betten im Zelt nur OK, wenn alle Teilnehmer sich gut verstehen. Vielleicht braucht man auch 2-Mann-Zelte?	(3)
What about the communal wash houses?	3 Klos und 2 Duschen sind zu wenig. Brauchen mindestens 4. Warmes Wasser aus Solaranlage prima.	(4)
Parents often worry about their children's safety. What information do you think we should give them to make sure they feel OK about this tour?	Elektrischer Zaun ums Lager, Nachtwache mit Gewehren, Sauberes Wasser aus eigenem Brunnen, Ranger gut ausgebildet, Elefanten zahm.	(5)

Green Line Oberstufe Klasse 10
ISBN: 978-3-12-560021-8

Topic 5 Make a difference

1 Listening: Fundraising

Either:
Some members of a youth group are talking about fundraising (raising money for charity). Answer the questions with not more than six words.

1. What charity are the youth group planning to raise funds for? ______________________
2. How much money did they make for charity last year? ______________________
3. How much money does Mike hope they can raise this year? ______________________
4. How has the club changed since last year? ______________________
5. What was the group's fundraising event last year? ______________________
6. Where did Jack hear about the idea of a hotdog-eating race? ______________________
7. Why mustn't the event cost much to set up? ______________________
8. According to Jack, what is another benefit of fundraising? ______________________
9. What four things does Amita suggest to give the event more publicity? ______________________ ______________________ ______________________
10. What decision does the group make about the fundraising event? ______________________

Or:
Some members of a youth group are talking about fundraising. Complete the table with the missing information.

Suggested fundraising event	Reasons for	Reasons against
(0) fun-run	easy to organize	did it last year other organisations have had them
cake sale	could make lots of money	most members of the group (1) ______________
hotdog-eating contest	fun	would give the wrong message because (2) ______________
trekking in Peru	exciting	(3) ______________
sponsored swim	(4) ______________	boring to watch
body painting	no reason given	(5) ______________
growing a (6) ______________	no reason given	not enough people in the group could grow one

Green Line Oberstufe Klasse 10
ISBN: 978-3-12-560021-8

2 Listening: Adam's story

Either:

Liz is doing an interview with Adam, a volunteer, for the school paper.
Listen and tick (✔) the correct answer. Only one is correct.

1. Where is Adam working as a volunteer?
   a) In a shelter for homeless people. ☐
   b) In a shop selling fruit and vegetables. ☐
   c) In an inner-city allotment garden. ☐

2. How did Adam feel when he looked at the photographs of criminals?
   a) He was shocked because they were his age. ☐
   b) He was angry about the number of young criminals in the area. ☐
   c) He was sorry that he had gone into that area at night. ☐

3. What made Adam first think about becoming a volunteer?
   a) He decided it would be useful for his future career. ☐
   b) He started to think about how lucky he was. ☐
   c) He wanted to help prevent street crime. ☐

4. What is the main aim of the volunteer project Adam is working on?
   a) To help people who don't have a place to live. ☐
   b) To look after parks in the city centre. ☐
   c) To raise money for charity. ☐

5. Who organizes the allotment garden project?
   a) A local social services worker. ☐
   b) An employee of the City Farm project. ☐
   c) The volunteers who work on the project. ☐

6. What kind of work does Adam want to do in the future?
   a) He wants to become a lawyer. ☐
   b) He wants to work in farming. ☐
   c) He wants to continue to work with homeless people. ☐

Or:

Listen to the interview with Adam, a volunteer.
Take notes to answer these questions.

1. What did Adam plan to become after university? ____________________
2. What happened to Adam after leaving the library? ____________________
3. Which three advantages of his own background ____________________
   does Adam mention? ____________________
4. Where is City Farm? ____________________
5. What used to be on the site of City Farm? ____________________
6. How many years has City Farm existed? ____________________
7. Who does the work on City Farm? ____________________
8. Who organizes the project? ____________________

Green Line Oberstufe Klasse 10
ISBN: 978-3-12-560021-8

3 Reading: Fixing a hole

I don't like the term 'guerrilla gardener'. For a start, the similarity in sound between 'guerilla' and 'gorilla' gives my friends endless inspiration for jokes. Why is it that some jokes just never seem to get old and die?

"Another gorilla garden, John? Is it full of banana trees? Ooh, ooh, ooh!"

Laugh? I almost did. The first time. More to the point, though, I don't like the term because it sounds a bit political. I don't go out in the middle of the night and make a flower garden in the middle of the building site for a new giant supermarket. I don't plant vegetables in land belonging to a factory. I think it's great people do those things, or at least, I think I think it's great, but that's not what I do. I'll explain how it started.

I was on my way home one evening, after dark. The road was wet, the lights on my bike aren't fantastic and I didn't see the pothole[1]. That was a mistake which cost me a broken wrist and a broken wheel. The broken wrist was painful and annoying, but at least getting it fixed was free. A new back wheel for the bike wasn't so easy, not for somebody who'd been unemployed for over a year.

Once my wrist was better, I had an idea. I made a little garden in the pothole. I took some earth and some plants from one of my window-boxes[2], and I put them in the pothole. Very nice they looked too. My thinking was that the flowers would warn people on their bikes about the pothole, and even if they didn't see it, filling it with earth would make it less likely that they'd have an accident.

Then I started thinking about the other potholes in my street. The road really isn't in very good condition and I decided to make gardens in all of them. My neighbours already thought I was a bit nuts[3], to be honest, and seeing me out there planting flowers in the middle of the road obviously didn't change their opinions about that, because none of them said anything about it. But other people coming down our street stopped, looked and asked me what I was doing, and why. Some of them even took photos.

When a car goes over a pothole garden, of course, there's not a lot left, but I've noticed that most drivers try not to run them over. They go around them, or drive carefully so the garden goes between the wheels. It certainly seems to slow them down – most of them actually obey the speed limit now. Anyway, after a while I noticed that the neighbours had started to get used to the idea, because I didn't always have to remake the damaged gardens. Sometimes I'd see that somebody else had done it. I even found plants in pots[4] left outside my door with notes saying things like "Keep up the good work". One Saturday night some kids destroyed most of the gardens. The next day, about ten of us were out there, putting them back again. Mr Evans at number 11 took us to the garden centre in his car and paid for some more plants.

"It's my treat[5]," he said. "Four of my numbers came up last month, and I won a few hundred."

Then there was the article in the local paper, followed by the report on the local TV news, followed by the article in a national paper.

I thought maybe there'd be something on the national TV, but then I realised I was being big-headed[6]. It's just a few flowers in some holes in the road.

When the lady from the council phoned, I was quite surprised. The news stories all mentioned that I was unemployed, but I didn't think anything of it. Half the people around here are unemployed. It's no big deal. She didn't offer me a job then and there. She just said she'd send me an application form for a job, but she was sure I'd be a strong candidate.

At the interview they liked what they called my initiative, and now here I am, one of the gardening team at the city zoo. I'm getting on quite well with the rest of the team, and yesterday Diana, who works in the café, said she'd seen me on the telly and gave me her e-mail address so I could send her some photos of the gardens. I'm not counting my chickens[7], but you never know. Miracles happen.

And yes, they do have gorillas here. Go on, enjoy yourself. I'll even pretend to laugh if you want me to.

[1] **pothole** hole in the surface of a road; [2] **window-box** box for planting flowers placed outside a window; [3] **nuts** crazy; [4] **pot** small container for growing plants; [5] **It's my treat** I'll pay for this; [6] **big-headed** conceited, thinking you are more important than you are; [7] **count your chickens (before they're hatched)** when you think you have something before you actually have it

Green Line Oberstufe Klasse 10
ISBN: 978-3-12-560021-8

Either:
Is the following information true, false or not in the text?

	true	false	not in text
1. John had an accident while riding his bike at night.			
2. At the time of his accident John hadn't had a job for more than a year.			
3. John wrote to the council to complain about the pothole.			
4. John bought flowers to put in his first pothole garden.			
5. At first, John's neighbours were annoyed about his project.			
6. One of John's neighbours won a lot of money on the lottery.			
7. John's pothole gardens were shown on national TV.			
8. At the time of writing the story, John is no longer unemployed.			

Or:
Read the text. Tick (✔) the correct answer to each question. Only one is correct.

1. How did John break his wrist?
   a) He was knocked over by a bike that went over a pothole. ☐
   b) His bike went over a pothole and he fell off. ☐
   c) A car knocked him into a pothole while he was riding his bike. ☐

2. What was the most annoying thing for John about his accident?
   a) He couldn't work while he was recovering. ☐
   b) His wrist took a long time to get better. ☐
   c) He had to pay for repairs to his bike. ☐

3. Why did John decide to start his project?
   a) To warn other road users about the potholes. ☐
   b) To develop his gardening skills. ☐
   c) To force the council to repair the roads. ☐

4. Why did John have to replace all the pothole gardens one weekend?
   a) Because they had been damaged by the traffic. ☐
   b) Because his neighbours complained. ☐
   c) Because they had been destroyed by teenagers. ☐

5. What other benefit of the pothole gardens mentioned in the text?
   a) The street looks more attractive. ☐
   b) People now drive more slowly. ☐
   c) There is more wildlife in the area. ☐

6. Why did the woman from the council phone John?
   a) She suggested a job for him to apply for. ☐
   b) She wanted to tell him about a television interview. ☐
   c) She wanted to offer him a job. ☐

7. What does John hope will happen soon?
   a) He hopes that he will appear on national television. ☐
   b) He hopes that he and Diana can start a relationship. ☐
   c) He would like to have permanent employment. ☐

Green Line Oberstufe Klasse 10
ISBN: 978-3-12-560021-8

Analysis:
Answer the questions.

1. *What can we infer about the narrator's attitude to politics?*

2. *From the text, what kind of activity is usually described as 'guerrilla gardening'?*

3. *How do the narrator's neighbours react?*

4. *What can we guess about the narrator's relationships with other people in general?*

5. *Give details of the narrator's use of humour.*

6. *What do we know about the neighbourhood where the narrator lives?*

7. *What double meaning can you find in the title?*

Green Line Oberstufe Klasse 10
ISBN: 978-3-12-560021-8

4 Reading: Protestors win a battle against development

Tonight will be a night of celebration for the campaigners at the Goscroft Nature Reserve[1]. The council's plans to build thousands of homes in the green belt[2] around Nettingford have now been stopped, after hundreds of local residents protested.

Goscroft Nature Reserve has been managed by local volunteers for over forty years. It provides a home for frogs, wild deer, foxes and rare birds. The bittern[3], one of the rarest birds in the UK, with fewer than 200 adult pairs in the whole country, has been seen at the site. The reserve also has a small but important community of endangered[4] red squirrels.

"It's an amazing place," said Harry Parker, a local resident who visits the reserve frequently. "Even though it's only three miles from the city, you can walk through ancient woodland and if you're lucky, bump into[5] some of the wildlife. I've been photographing wildlife here ever since the place first opened as a reserve. The animals need the fields around the reserve to feed. If a whole town of new houses were built there, there's no way that most of these animals could survive in a tiny pocket of woodland.

My grandchildren would never be able to get to see this pretty place. It's a fragile[6] natural space and it would be all too easy to lose it forever. I was amazed when I first heard that they were planning to build right next to the reserve. I mean, if they're allowed to build here, they could build anywhere at all." Jane Marshall, one of 700 or more people actively protesting against the plans during the two year campaign, reacted to today's decision.

"I simply couldn't believe it when I read about what they were planning to do. I was furious. At a time when people don't have much money to spend, the council wants to build thousands of new homes. We would be left with a lot of houses that nobody could afford in an area that was no longer beautiful. This is not just about the wildlife. It's about democracy and our right to say what is really important about the place we live in. I'd have felt angry about this forever if we hadn't been able to save this area for the sake of the next generation. But today's decision just shows what people-power can do. We made a difference. I'm proud to have been a part of this campaign."

The council insists that it needs 26,000 new homes over the next twenty years to meet the demand from local families. Local MP, Sheila Smith disagrees with the council's policy. "I'm delighted[7] to hear about the decision. There are lots of brown-field sites[8] that could be developed without eating into the green belt. We need to look at ways to encourage builders to redevelop unused industrial sites before we start building on green-field sites. There are empty factories and industrial buildings which would make good sites for development.

I think the council didn't understand the importance of this countryside for the people and they should learn from this campaign by giving the environment a higher priority."

But the battle isn't over yet. "It's great news, of course." says Sheila. "However, although we've won this particular campaign, the need for new homes hasn't gone away. There are other areas that the council will be looking at as possible sites for building. What we need to do is to make sure that new plans respect our open spaces. If we don't fight to protect what we've got, it'll be lost forever."

[1]**nature reserve** an area reserved for plants and wildlife;
[2]**green belt** an area of open land around a city where building is forbidden or controlled;
[3]**bittern** a rare type of water bird; [4]**endangered** at risk of becoming extinct;
[5]**bump into** meet, encounter; [6]**fragile** delicate, easily broken;
[7]**delighted** very pleased; [8]**brown-field sites** land previously used for industrial purposes

Green Line Oberstufe Klasse 10
ISBN: 978-3-12-560021-8

Either:
Read the text. Tick (✔) the correct answer to each question. Only one is correct.

1. What is the main subject of the article?
   a) The best way to organise protest campaigns. ☐
   b) The importance of nature reserves near large cities. ☐
   c) The defeat of a plan to build in an environmentally important area. ☐

2. Which of these reasons **isn't** given for the reserve's importance?
   a) It's a home for wild animals. ☐
   b) It's a good place for children to learn about the environment. ☐
   c) It's near a large city. ☐

3. Why does Harry believe the wildlife wouldn't survive if the houses were built?
   a) Because then there wouldn't be enough land where they could find food. ☐
   b) Because they would be killed by traffic. ☐
   c) Because the noise of the people in the houses would frighten them away from. the area. ☐

4. How does Jane Marshall sum up the campaign?
   a) Politicians aren't interested in beauty or nature. ☐
   b) New homes aren't necessary in this area. ☐
   c) The decision is a victory for democracy. ☐

5. What mistake does Sheila Smith say the council planners made?
   a) They didn't think people would care so much about the countryside. ☐
   b) They should have planned to build houses further away from the town. ☐
   c) They acted too quickly. ☐

6. How does she think that the council planners should act differently in the future?
   a) They need to involve local businesses more. ☐
   b) They should give more publicity to the importance of the environment. ☐
   c) Whenever possible they should choose areas which are not green fields to build on. ☐

Or:
Read the newspaper article. Is the following information true, false or not in the text? Tick (✔) the right box.

	true	false	not in the text
1. Most of the work on the reserve is done by volunteers.			
2. The council plans to build 26,000 homes around Nettingford in the next twenty years.			
3. Developers are angry about the decision to stop the building project.			
4. There are about 400 bitterns living at the Goscroft Nature Reserve.			
5. Harry Parker is a professional photographer for the reserve.			
6. There is enough food inside the reserve for the wildlife to survive.			
7. Jane Marshall says she feels helpless to change anything.			
8. Sheila Smith thinks that the council made mistakes.			
9. After this decision the protestors don't need to worry about further building projects.			

Green Line Oberstufe Klasse 10
ISBN: 978-3-12-560021-8

Analysis:
Answer the questions.

1. *Is the article neutral? Why?/Why not?*

____

____

____

2. *What is the style of the text? Where could you find such an article?*

____

____

____

3. *What emotions do the speakers show? Give examples from the text.*

____

____

____

4. *"If they are allowed to build here, they could build anywhere." In your own words, explain what Harry Parker means.*

____

____

____

5. *Why does Jane Marshall say that this is a bad time for new building development?*

____

____

____

6. *Explain the metaphor 'the battle isn't over yet'.*

____

____

____

____

Green Line Oberstufe Klasse 10
ISBN: 978-3-12-560021-8

5 Understanding films: Barefoot College

Either:
Watch the film. Are these statements true or false? Tick (✔) the right box.

	true	false
1. The report is about an unusual approach to education in Asia.		
2. The children's parliament is an exam for the students of the college.		
3. The students have some control over how the college is organized.		
4. Many of the students at the college both study and work.		
5. The majority of students at the college are under 13.		
6. All the students at Barefoot College speak the same language.		
7. The students at the college come from several different countries.		
8. here are different areas for different castes to eat in.		
9. There are more than twenty Barefoot Colleges in India today.		
10. Former students from the college spread the idea of equality in villages all over the world.		

Or:
Watch the film and take notes to answer these questions.

1. *What surprised the presenter about the children's parliament in comparison with Britain?*

2. *When do the students usually study?*

3. *What are the women in the video learning and why is this particularly useful?*

4. *Comment on this phrase: "So much for the old stereotype that technical skills are strictly a man's domain."*

5. *What does the narrator say is the main lesson learnt in the Barefoot College?*

6. *What is Munkabi's position in the school?*

7. *What does Munkabi think will help to make things better in the long term?*

Green Line Oberstufe Klasse 10
ISBN: 978-3-12-560021-8

6 Writing: A post

A post on an Internet forum:

> What's the point in trying to change the world? You can't do anything on your own, and anyway, it's not our responsibility. We elect governments, and it's their job to solve the world's problems.

Write a reply discussing the topic of this post. Write about 150 words.

- Explain the message the writer wants to convey.
- Argue against the message, and support your argument with examples.
- Offer an alternative message.

7 Writing: Children in Bangladesh

Millions of children in Bangladesh can't go to their local school because they work full time, many of them in factories making clothes and other products for Western countries. Some of these working children receive a basic education from UCEP (Underprivileged Children's Educational Programs). They come to lessons for three hours before or after work.

Write a report discussing the information in the statistics. Write about 150 words.

- Present the situation shown in the photo and the text.
- Suggest at least one way to improve the situation.

Green Line Oberstufe Klasse 10
ISBN: 978-3-12-560021-8

8 Speaking: Developing countries

Part 1: Interview:

1. Think of your last visit to the dentist and describe your treatment.
2. Would you visit a developing country? Why? / Why not?
3. What differences would you expect there to be between 'developing' and 'developed' countries?

Part 2: Individual long turn

Student A: *Describe and analyse picture 1 based on your knowledge of problems in the developing world.*

Student B: *Describe and analyse picture 2 based on your knowledge of problems in the developing world.*

Picture 1

Picture 2

Part 3: Discussion

Student A: *Your best friend wants to spend ten months working on a volunteer programme in Africa. The job is working as an assistant in a mobile clinic. Discuss the pros and cons of going on this type of programme.*

Student B: *You want to spend ten months working on a volunteer programme in Africa. The job is working as an assistant in a mobile clinic. Present your arguments for choosing this job.*

Green Line Oberstufe Klasse 10
ISBN: 978-3-12-560021-8

9 Speaking: Protest

Part 1: Interview:

1. Have you ever seen a demonstration? What was it about?
2. Have you ever been on a demonstration? Why did you go?
3. If you've never been on a demonstration would you go on one? Why? / Why not? (What would the reason for the demonstration have to be for you to go?)
4. Why do you think people go on demonstrations?

Part 2: Individual long turn

Student A: *Describe cartoon 1 and comment on it.*

Student B: *Describe cartoon 2 and comment on it.*

Cartoon 1

Cartoon 2

Part 3: Discussion

Student A: *You are of the opinion that demonstrating is a waste of time, and achieves very little.*

Student B: *You are of the opinion that demonstrating isn't a waste of time, and can make a significant difference.*

Green Line Oberstufe Klasse 10
ISBN: 978-3-12-560021-8

10 Mediation: A summary

You picked up this leaflet when you visited a Fair Trade shop in Ireland. You want to use it to explain to a friend why you think she should buy Fair Trade products whenever possible.
As this friend doesn't speak English very well, you summarize the main arguments of the article for her in German.

One Earth

Wholefood and Healthfoods Store
17 Jameston Street, Cork, co. Cork, Ireland. Tel. 021 477821

www.oneearthcork.info

Fairtrade at One Earth

Here at One Earth, we are very proud to support the Fairtrade Foundation. You probably already know about Fairtrade tea, coffee and chocolate, and understand why it's important to pay a fair price to farmers in developing countries. But there's much more to Fairtrade than paying a few extra cents when you a buy a packet of coffee so the people who grew the beans earn enough money to live. Here are some things you may not know.

- Many other products from developing countries are available with the Fairtrade guarantee that producers receive a fair price. Clothes, flowers, soap, fruit, breakfast, cereals, sweets, ice-cream and wine are just a few of the things that can now be bought with the Fairtrade symbol.
- Fairtrade isn't just about paying a little more to poor farmers. Local buyers must always pay at least the Fairtrade minimum price. This guarantees farmers a certain level of money for their produce, they can invest in education, healthcare, clean water and other things which benefit the whole community, not just the farmers themselves.
- In order to meet Fairtrade standards, companies which hire workers have to prove that all the extra money they receive is spent on benefits for the workers, and that how that money is spent is decided by the workers. Fairtrade also protects the rights of the workers according to the standards of the International Labour Organisation. This means working conditions must be safe, there must be no discrimination and no child labour. One of the most recent additions is Fairtrade jewellery: jewellery made with gold that has been mined in safe conditions by adults.
- Fairtrade doesn't just benefit a few lucky communities. The lives of millions of people in the developing world have been improved. Around the world there are children in schools, doctors treating patients in clinics and workers who have not died in accidents thanks to Fairtrade. This is possible because millions of people in developed countries have chosen to buy Fairtrade. There are even Fairtrade Towns – at present 750 towns and cities, including Rome, San Francisco and London. These towns and cities make sure that local schools, hospitals, council offices etc., are supplied with Fairtrade products as much as possible.

Green Line Oberstufe Klasse 10
ISBN: 978-3-12-560021-8

11 Mediation: Exchanging information

Your cousin Sheila from Canada is staying at your house.
Your friend Frank is going to run in a marathon to raise money for charity.
Frank wants to ask Sheila to contribute some money, but he doesn't speak English very well. Help to communicate between him and Sheila.

Frank: Ich werde an einem Benefiz-Marathon in Barcelona teilnehmen. Hast du vielleicht Lust mich zu sponsern?

You: (1) ______________________________

____

Sheila: Which charity is the marathon supporting?

You: (2) ______________________________

____

Frank: Es geht nicht um Spenden für eine bestimmte Organisation. Jeder Läufer entscheidet selbst, welche Organisation er unterstützt. Ich sammle für Ärzte ohne Grenzen (Médecins Sans Frontiers). Sie entsenden Ärzte und liefern medizinische Geräte in Entwicklungsländer – besonders dorthin, wo gerade Krieg ist.

You: (3) ______________________________

____

____

____

Sheila: Yes, I know who they are. But how does you running a marathon help?

You: (4) ______________________________

____

____

Frank: Das Prinzip ist einfach. Du gibst mir eine kleine Spende und ich verspreche im Gegenzug den Marathon zu beenden und das Geld zu spenden.

You: (5) ______________________________

____

____

Sheila: Hmm. But you'll have to fly to Barcelona and stay in a hotel. Won't I just be paying for you to have a nice holiday with a bit of running in the middle?

You: (6) ______________________________

____

____

Green Line Oberstufe Klasse 10
ISBN: 978-3-12-560021-8

Frank: Nein! Die Kosten trage ich selbst. Ich werde nicht fliegen und in einem Hotel übernachten. Ich fahre mit dem Bus und zelte auf einem Campingplatz außerhalb der Stadt.

You: (7) ______________________________

____

____

Sheila: How much do I have to give?

You: (8) ______________________________

Frank: Das ist deine Entscheidung. Jeder Euro hilft.

You: (9) ______________________________

Sheila: OK. Put me down for five euros then.

You: (10) ______________________________

Frank: Danke! Die sind garantiert gut angelegt. Ich habe gelesen, dass Ärzte ohne Grenzen (Médecins Sans Frontiers) sehr effizient arbeitet. Die Ausgaben für Verwaltung und Spendenaktionen sind gering. So kommt fast das gesamte Geld ihrer eigentlichen Arbeit zu gute.

You: (11) ______________________________

____

____

____

Sheila: Really? I didn't know that. Make it ten, then. They do very good work and I can afford it. I'm going back to Canada next week, so it's probably easiest if I give it to you now. Here you are.

You: (12) ______________________________

____

____

____

Frank: Oh, das ist nett von dir! Danke.

You: (13) ______________________________

Sheila: No problem. Enjoy your trip to Barcelona. I was there a couple of years ago. It's a wonderful city.

You: (14) ______________________________

____

____

Green Line Oberstufe Klasse 10
ISBN: 978-3-12-560021-8

Topic 1 Growing up

1 Language in use: A Sicilian childhood

You're going to read a text about Lucia and her memories of growing up in a town in Sicily in the 1950s. Some words or phrases are missing from the text. Choose the correct answer (A, B, C or D) for each gap (1–10) in the text. Write your answers in the boxes provided. The first one (0) has been done for you.

Even though I'd describe my own childhood as peaceful, I … **(0)** admit that my parents were … **(1)** strict. The city of Catania in the period after the war was … **(2)** from being the kind of place where girls were encouraged to have their own ideas or ambitions.

To … **(3)** the truth, my father was an … **(4)** jealous man, with old-fashioned ideas. My father would never … **(5)** allow me to leave the family home alone. I couldn't go out because boys would talk to me when I walked down the street. I couldn't take any risks or … **(6)** any decisions for myself. My father was … **(7)** telling me what I couldn't do. I ached with boredom. As I grew older, life with my protective father became … **(8)** impossible to put up with, and the arguments grew worse and worse.

… **(9)**, I was looking for an opportunity to get away from home. Shortly before my sixteenth birthday, while visiting a school friend, I met a man called Marco who was much older than myself. He was rich, twenty-eight years old and worked in the coffee business. Optimistically, I told myself this would be my escape route. I could marry and have a place of my own and some freedom at last. … **(10)**, that didn't quite work out as I'd planned.

	A	B	C	D
0	myself ✔	personally	basically	much
1	actually	absolutely	obviously	incredibly
2	mostly	more than ever	very far	unfortunately
3	make	speak	say	tell
4	absolutely	extremely	exactly	entirely
5	more	far	even	so
6	break	do	have	make
7	always	himself	extremely	really
8	hopefully	honestly	completely	very
9	Exactly	Basically	Extremely	Immediately
10	Especially	Badly	Hardly	Unfortunately

0	1	2	3	4	5	6	7	8	9	10
A										

Green Line Oberstufe Klasse 10
ISBN: 978-3-12-560021-8

2 Language in use: The golden age of childhood

You are going to read a text about childhood. Replace the adverbs or adverbial phrases in bold print (1–10) with an adverb from the list below. Write your answers in the spaces provided at the end of the text. The first one (0) has been done for you.

actually • completely • constantly • eventually • fast • frankly • nearly • apparently • obviously • recently • responsibly

(0) It seems that every generation believes that the period when they themselves were children is the golden age of childhood. Some adults talk of a time when children were **(1) entirely** free to play outdoors without parents **(2) endlessly** worrying about their safety. **(3) Clearly** this dream of a childhood of delicious home-cooked food and home-made entertainment is a myth. In Britain today, more children than ever before can grow up in safety and comfort, with plenty of food, health care and education. But are children now growing up too **(4) quickly** and spending too much time in front of their computers?

A report published **(5) a short time ago** reveals that **(6) almost** half of British children use social networking sites like Facebook. Many parents are worried and think that their children are spending too much time looking at their computer screens and not enough time **(7) really** playing with their friends face-to-face. Gina Taylor, a child psychologist says, "**(8) To be honest**, I think parents should control the amount of time their children spend on the Internet. It's not fair to expect a ten-year-old to act **(9) in a mature way** about things like this. **(10) In the end**, it will lead to problems."

0 Apparently

1 ____________

2 ____________

3 ____________

4 ____________

5 ____________

6 ____________

7 ____________

8 ____________

9 ____________

10 ____________

Green Line Oberstufe Klasse 10
ISBN: 978-3-12-560021-8

Topic 2 Multi-ethnic Britain

1 Language in use: Potential dangers

*The text below is a comment from an Internet blog about multi-ethnic Britain. Complete the sentences with the verbs in **bold print** (1-10). Decide whether to use -ing-forms or infinitives. Write your answers in the spaces provided at the end of the text. The first one (0) has been done for you.*

First I would like **(0) say** that I have nothing against people **(1) want** to better their own lives or the lives of their family. But if you are going to make the life- **(2) change** decision to emigrate to another country, you should be able **(3) speak** the language. Multiculturalism has the potential **(4) divide** whole communities. I think not **(5) speak** the same language causes problems. There is also the issue of **(6) take** care of a population which is growing too fast. Immigration and the freedom of the Internet has enabled other cultures **(7) influence** our art, music, fashion, film and food. But **(8) choose** to encourage a respect for other cultures while **(9) deny** that Britain has its own, is wrong. **(10) tolerate** other cultures is the essence of liberal multiculturalism.

0 to say

1 ______________________ 6 ______________________

2 ______________________ 7 ______________________

3 ______________________ 8 ______________________

4 ______________________ 9 ______________________

5 ______________________ 10 ______________________

Green Line Oberstufe Klasse 10
ISBN: 978-3-12-560021-8

2 Language in use: Nomads in Britain

You are going to read a text about Irish Travellers in the UK. Some words are missing from the text. Use the words below to complete each gap (1–10) in the text. Write your answers in the spaces provided at the end of the text. The first one (0) has been done for you.

mainstream • conditions • discriminated • fail • ethic • residents • abuse • forced • glare at • perceived

In the middle of West London, there is … **(0)** with some neighbours. About 20 Irish Traveller families have been living in mobile homes for the past 20 years. The … **(1)** here are not very good at all.

"To be honest, I don't really like the environment around here", says Terry O'Leary, one of the … **(2)**. Irish Travellers don't look different to English people, but in the UK they have been recognized as an … **(3)** minority – with their own culture, traditions and language.

When asked how the travellers are … **(4)** by other members of society, Terry replies "Some people … **(5)** to understand us and many people … **(6)** me. We also suffer … **(7)** from people who don't understand us," says Terry. "I feel that we're … **(8)** against for living the way we want to live."

Terry works hard and could easily buy a house but says that for most Travellers it is all about their family and traditions, and that he would never become … **(9)**.

"I'll never be … **(10)** into a house, I love the site. I lived in a house for a year and I hated it. A house is like a prison."

0 tension

1 ____________ 6 ____________

2 ____________ 7 ____________

3 ____________ 8 ____________

4 ____________ 9 ____________

5 ____________ 10 ____________

Green Line Oberstufe Klasse 10
ISBN: 978-3-12-560021-8

Topic 3 The Blue Planet

1 Language in use: Smog

*You are going to read a text about smog. Some words are missing from the text. Use the correct form of the words in **bold print** to complete each gap (1-10) in the text. Write your answers in the spaces provided at the end of the text. The first one (0) has been done for you.*

SMOG

Smog is one of the most common **(0) environment** problems in the world today and is one of the worst things that people living in **(1) industry** cities have to deal with. Smog is made up of over one hundred chemicals, including carbon monoxide and ozone, and the effect of these when mixed with sunlight can be very **(2) power**.
Cars, fires, waste treatment, oil **(3) produce** and paints all cause smog, and gas from petrol stations and car engines send **(4) poison** gases into the air, making the problem worse. Many people living in cities are **(5) aware** that their health issues, including coughing, sore throats, chest pains and breathing problems, are caused by **(6) pollute** and smog, but governments are slowly realising that something needs to be done. Laws are being introduced to support the **(7) develop** of cars that produce less smog, and to encourage chemical companies to be more **(8) effect** in producing less dangerous chemicals. Also, some local communities are now making great efforts by, for example, reducing their use of dangerous products such as barbecues, house paint and kitchen cleaners and some local governments are asking people to car-share or use bikes to travel to work or school.
For many of us, the need to recycle and to use **(9) renew** energy are issues we hear about every day. There is no **(10) short** of issues that need our urgent attention. Now we must hope that the reduction of smog can be added to the list.

0 environmental

1 ______________ 6 ______________

2 ______________ 7 ______________

3 ______________ 8 ______________

4 ______________ 9 ______________

5 ______________ 10 ______________

Green Line Oberstufe Klasse 10
ISBN: 978-3-12-560021-8

2 Language in use: Pandas

You are going to read an article in which a naturalist gives his opinion on pandas and how far we should go to save them. Some words are missing from the text. Choose the correct answer (A, B or C) for each gap (1 – 10) in the text. Write your answers in the boxes provided. The first one (0) has been done for you.

I don't want the panda to die out, and I hate to think that it is at … **(0)**. I want all … **(1)** to stay alive – that's why I get up in the morning. I don't even kill mosquitoes or flies. So if pandas … **(2)** in the long term, that would be great but, let's face it, there isn't enough money to … **(3)** all animals in danger and I think we're going to have to make some hard choices.

The truth is, pandas are extraordinarily expensive to keep going. We spend millions and millions of pounds on them when really the best thing we could do would be to look after those parts of the world with the greatest biodiversity. Without … **(4)**, you've got nothing, so maybe if we took all the money we spend on pandas and used it to stop the … **(5)** to the rainforest, we might be doing a better job.

Of course, it's easier to raise money for something attractive. Charismatic animals like pandas do appeal to people's emotional side, and attract a lot of public attention. But they focus on just one animal. This … **(6)** began in the 1970s with 'Save the Tiger', 'Save the Panda', 'Save the Whale', and so on, and it is now out of date. I think pandas have played a valuable role up to now in … **(7)** the profile of conservation, but perhaps it's time to move on.

Panda conservationists may stand up and say, "It's such a well-loved species and we're also conserving the Chinese forest at the same time." And when that works, I'm not against it. But we have to accept that some animals are stronger than others and some might not be worth saving. Pandas have an extremely limited … **(8)** and get ill very easily.

… **(9)** is very much a part of life on earth. And we are going to have to get used to it in the next few years because global … **(10)** is going to result in all sorts of disappearances. I believe we should now be spreading our net more widely and looking after the areas where these animals live. This way, we can preserve as much of life as we possibly can, using hard science to make educated decisions as to which species are most important to a community's maintenance.

'Save the Rainforest', or 'Save the Kalahari' – that would be better.

	A	B	C
0	danger	risk ✔	problem
1	species	breeds	types
2	stayed	survived	remained
3	protect	keep	preserve
4	surroundings	home	territory
5	damage	injury	pollution
6	way	idea	project
7	raising	lifting	rising
8	food	diet	menu
9	removal	disappearance	extinction
10	heating	warming	temperature

0	1	2	3	4	5	6	7	8	9	10
B										

Green Line Oberstufe Klasse 10
ISBN: 978-3-12-560021-8

Topic 4 South Africa

1 Language in use: South Africa

Here is a short extract about the variety of languages in South Africa. Choose prepositions to fill the gaps (1 – 10) in the text. The first one (0) has been done for you.

… **(0)** South Africa I experienced a multicultural situation. The country is home … **(1)** many different groups. South Africans are descended … **(2)** African, Asian and European immigrants and speak a variety … **(3)** languages. The majority … **(4)** people speak English and this helps them to communicate … **(5)** one another. Some people worry … **(6)** their children, as they no longer pay attention … **(7)** their home language and their cultural roots. English should never take the place … **(8)** other languages. I believe all eleven official languages should be supported … **(9)** the families and used … **(10)** schools.

0 In ________ 1 ________ 2 ________ 3 ________

4 ________ 5 ________ 6 ________ 7 ________

8 ________ 9 ________ 10 ________

2 Language in use: The new South Africa

This text tells how South African politics changed in 1994. Find a word with the same meaning for each phrase in **bold print***. The first one (0) has been done for you.*

Before 1994 the South African government did not respect the rights of all its … **(0) people living in the country**. South Africa has been a … **(1) government elected by the people** since April the 27th, 1994. That was when a … **(2) larger part** of the population voted for Nelson Mandela as president. They no longer wanted a government that believed in … **(3) enforced racial separation.** Most South Africans celebrated their … **(4) experience of becoming** free with a party. They were now all … **(5) the same** before the law.

0 citizens ________ 1 ________ 2 ________

3 ________ 4 ________ 5 ________

3 Language in use: A better future for all

You are going to read a text about a better future for young people. In every sentence there's a word which expresses possibility. Find it and write it in the space provided after each line. The first one has been done for you.

You probably worry about the future of children in Africa.	0	probably
Perhaps the future won't be so bad for the youth of South Africa.	1	
With a good education they could get good jobs.	2	
Education might also help to prevent HIV and AIDS.	3	
I think you would agree with me.	4	
No child in Africa should go hungry.	5	

Green Line Oberstufe Klasse 10
ISBN: 978-3-12-560021-8

2 Language in use: Tips for the trip

This text is about preparing for a trip to South Africa. Some words are missing from the text. Choose the correct answer (A, B, or C) for each gap (1 – 10) in the text. Write your answers in the boxes provided. The first one has been done for you.

When I heard that you're going to South Africa, I could hardly take … **(0)** the information. You're lucky that you can take … **(1)** the offer of a tour to South Africa. Don't go … **(2)** a guide book that will help you to get … **(3)** the local culture. You should definitely take … **(4)** the tour agency's invitation to visit a game park. Remember, if you put … **(5)** your packing for too long, you'll get … **(6)** a terrible muddle when the time comes to leave. It's also a good idea to put … **(7)** some warm clothes that you can put … **(8)** if the weather turns cold. When you get … **(9)** the airport, check in at the information desk and find out when your plane will take … **(10)**.

	A	B	C
0	in ✔	up	off
1	in	up	off
2	on	without	into
3	to	up to	into
4	in	up	off
5	off	in	on
6	to	up to	into
7	off	in	on
8	off	in	on
9	to	down	at
10	up	off	on

0	1	2	3	4	5	6	7	8	9	10
A										

Green Line Oberstufe Klasse 10
ISBN: 978-3-12-560021-8

Topic 5 Make a difference

1 Language in use: Warm hearts, cold feet

You are going to read a magazine article about a local charity event. Choose the correct answer (A, B, C or D) for each gap (1 – 10) in the text. Write your answers in the boxes below. The first one (0) has been done for you.

Warm hearts, cold feet: the Wisconsin Polar Plunge

Phil Karpovsky stood near the lakeside and … **(0)** out at the water. The wind … **(1)** and it was just starting to snow a little. He was wearing a new suit, thick glasses and a tie and looked just like any other businessman.

Then he … **(2)** off his jacket, shirt, trousers and tie and threw his glasses down next to his clothes on the beach. Under his suit, he was wearing a Superman outfit. Then he … **(3)** down to the freezing lake and jumped in, landing next to other superheroes, teddy bears and girls in bikinis. Phil's two daughters cheered and his wife took photographs, as this year's Wisconsin Polar Plunge … **(4)**.

The event … **(5)** a lot since it started eight years ago. On the first Polar Plunge, 40 people went into the water for charity. This year more than 800 people took part in the event. Last year's plunge … **(6)** more than $17,000 dollars for the Special Olympics, and it is hoped that this year will make even more.

"This is the third time I … **(7)** this, now,' said Phil, after his icy swim. "I … **(8)** for weeks. It felt terrible when I first … **(9)** the water, but now I … (10) pretty good. It gives me a good feeling to see all these people down here doing this crazy thing for a great cause!"

	A	B	C	D
0	looked ✔	look	has looked	looking
1	blows	has blown	was blowing	blew
2	has pulled	pulled	pulls	was pulling
3	was running	has run	ran	has been running
4	is beginning	began	has begun	has been beginning
5	was growing	has grown	pollution	grows
6	was making	has made	made	has been making
7	did	was doing	've done	've been doing
8	'm preparing	prepare	've prepared	've been preparing
9	hit	am hitting	was hitting	have hit
10	feel	'm feeling	've been feeling	felt

0	1	2	3	4	5	6	7	8	9	10
A										

Green Line Oberstufe Klasse 10
ISBN: 978-3-12-560021-8

2 Language in use: The gift of a lifetime

You are going to read a short blog entry. Some words are missing from the text. Complete each gap (1 – 10) in the text using one word. Write your answers on the lines at the end of the text. The first one (0) has been done for you.

I know this is going to sound silly, but the person who has … (0) the most difference to me in my life so far is my twin sister. You … **(1)** probably thinking that of course my twin is going to … **(2)** some influence on me … **(3)** some way. My sister and I have always … **(4)** close of course; we believe … **(5)** the same things, we both have very strong views … **(6)** the way to make cheese on toast and we are both passionate … **(7)** music. But this is deeper than that. My sister is part of my life in a completely different way.

My sister has actually saved my life. I was a normal healthy thirteen-year-old when I started to get sick. After a few months of tests, the doctors told me that there was a problem with my kidneys[1]. I'd never really been ill much before, so the trips to the hospital and the treatments were difficult to get used to. Nothing seemed to work, one thing led … **(8)** another and I completely depended … **(9)** drugs and medical treatments to keep me going.

Then, one day, just before our fourteenth birthday, my sister sat down next to me and said she'd been speaking to my doctors.

'You know I said I was going to buy you a phone for your birthday?' she said. 'Well, I've decided to give you something else instead! I'm giving you a kidney.'

Well, you can see us now, so you can guess how things turned out! In fact, we're taking … **(10)** in a sponsored run to … **(11)** money for kidney research tomorrow. Wish us luck and if you want to … **(12)** a donation[2], that would be great, too!

[1]**kidneys** Nieren; [2]**donation** Spende

0 made

1 ______________ 6 ______________

2 ______________ 7 ______________

3 ______________ 8 ______________

4 ______________ 9 ______________

5 ______________ 10 ______________

Green Line Oberstufe Klasse 10
ISBN: 978-3-12-560021-8

Lösungen Topics

Topic 1 Growing up

1 Reading: A book review

Either:

a) 1. false; 2. false; 3. true; 4. true; 5. true; 6. false; 7. true; 8. true; 9. false; 10. true

b) 1. The book is set in South Wales. 2. Only the first part of the book is about the father. 6. She doesn't mention the style of the book. 9. She's looking forward to seeing the film.

Or:
1. b; 2. a; 3. a; 4. c; 5. b; 6. c

Tapescript:
Diesen Text finden Sie auf der CD-ROM.

2 Listening: Summer camp

Either:
1. tents; 2. apartment; 3. cook her own meals; 4. dining hall; 5. art; 6. music; 7. French; 8. grandparents

Or:
Lösungsvorschlag:
1. She would travel by train. 2. The brochure is still in its envelope / where her mother left it. 3. She's interested in painting, drawing and playing the guitar / arts and music. 4. She spends a lot of time talking to her friends on Facebook. 5. Because Elena speaks French very well. 6. Elena's mother has already bought it.

Tapescript:
Diesen Text finden Sie auf der CD-ROM.

3 Reading: Harriet's box of treasures

Either:
1. b; 2. c; 3. a; 4. c; 5. b; 6. a; 7. c

Or:
1. true; 2. not in the text (We only know that Harriet had loved him.) 3. true; 4. false (She says that Mrs Elton is 'very bad-tempered and disagreeable'.) 5. false (It was Harriet's.) 6. true; 7. not in the text (We only know that she finds it strange and amusing.) 8. not in the text; 9. false (Emma seems more mature and sensible than Harriet.) 10. true

Analysis:
1. It's clear that Harriet believed she was in love with Mr Elton, but he didn't share these feelings. From this passage, it's unclear whether Mr Elton knew of Harriet's feelings at the time, but Emma and Harriet have obviously spoken about the subject before. Since then Mr Elton has married someone else and hurt Harriet's feelings.
2. By changing the tense of the verb when she talks about the objects, Harriet shows that she is trying to move away from her earlier strong feelings. Her interest in Mr Elton and everything connected with him is still very fresh in her mind but she is trying to distance herself from them.
3. *Her curiosity was greatly excited.* (line 32)
   Emma was quite eager to see this superior treasure. (line 63)
   By describing Emma's interest, the author builds up the reader's interest in the contents of the parcel.
4. Harriet uses long sentences with lots of commas and extra information. This style is typical of many novels of this period. Sometimes Harriet's style of speech seems quite unstructured and disorganised, especially when she contradicts or corrects herself. This gives the reader the impression Harriet has a disorganised mind, and is ruled more by her feelings than by her mind.
5. In this passage, the author uses contrasts to create comic effects. One example of this is when Harriet describes everyday objects as 'valuable', 'treasures' and 'relics'. This increases the comic effect, when the reader becomes aware of exactly how trivial the objects in Harriet's box are. At the end of the passage, Harriet says very seriously, *There it goes, and there is an end, thank Heaven, of Mr Elton!* In Harriet's view of events this is an important event, but in reality she's just throwing some rubbish onto the fire. The contrast between Emma's cool amusement and Harriet's strong feelings also adds to the comic effect.
6. It's a light and humorous look at the way young people can persuade themselves that they're in love and that unimportant things are part of the romantic drama.

4 Reading: The adolescent brain

Either:
Paragraph 1, D:
Research may explain misunderstandings
Paragraph 2, F:
Post-adolescent brain development
Paragraph 3, A:
The brain gradually becomes more efficient
Paragraph 4, C:
Don't delay learning life skills
Paragraph 5, B:
Time to rethink educational policy?
(E is unused:
Brain development stops at adolescence)

Or:
1. false (The article shows that there's strong medical evidence to explain this difference.) 2. false (The human brain doesn't completely finish developing until we reach our early twenties.) 3. true; 4. false (Teenagers' brains have more connections and more grey matter than adult brains.) 5. true; 6. not in the text; 7. false (It becomes easier to think analytically and unemotionally in adult life.) 8. not in the text; 9. true; 10. true

Green Line Oberstufe Klasse 10
ISBN: 978-3-12-560021-8

Analysis:
1. Adults usually think teenagers are unreasonable and ruled more by their feelings than by their minds. The phrases *irrational and over-emotional behaviour in teenagers* and *getting angry about nothing* reflect the traditional view of teenage behaviour.
2. It was generally believed that the human brain was fully developed by the age of twelve. It now appears that the brain carries on changing and developing until we are twenty or older.
3. Between the ages of 12 and 20, the brain becomes more efficient. Frequently-used connections become stronger and less-used connections die off.
4. The writer uses a contrast to compare the two different thought processes. The reader is asked to imagine two different locations to read a poem: a quiet library and a noisy café. The contrast helps to show the difficulties that teenagers experience when they are asked to do an analytical task.
5. According to the article, it is important that teenagers learn the life skills they need during adolescence, because after they reach their twenties their learning will not be so effective.
6. The writer suggests that it would be a good idea to think about changing the way teenagers are educated, with more emphasis on making decisions and solving problems.
7. *Lösungsvorschlag:* Teenagers don't only develop their skills and abilities through academic study. Social and creative leisure activities also play an important part in their development. In my opinion, teenagers should have more control over how they spend their time, and have more freedom to concentrate on the things that most interest them.

5 Understanding films: Discrimination

a) 1. b; 2. c; 3. a; 4. b; 5. c; 6. b

b) *Lösungsvorschlag:*
1. The main point is that even though there is no evidence to show that young black men are more likely to commit crimes than young white men, they are arrested or stopped and searched far more often.
2. The outreach programme is trying to give young black people the chance to avoid getting involved in the criminal justice system.
3. The police officer said that the police had recognised the part played in the problem by stop-and-search and had taken firm action. They welcomed the call for a wider debate and more research into the causes.
4. The young man in the hat blames the general public. The man in the café thinks people are responsible for their own actions. The boy blames politics and the government. Claudia accuses the police and the criminal justice system of racism and inequality.
5. She means that the inequality isn't just because a few people in the criminal justice system are racist, but because the whole criminal justice system is unjust and unequal.
6. The variety of people and places gives the impression of a balanced and thorough piece of reporting. It also makes it more interesting to watch and listen to.

Transcript:
Diesen Text finden Sie auf der CD-ROM.

6 Writing: An article

Lösungsvorschlag:
The cartoon appears to be set in a typical family home and shows a father sitting at a table watching his son doing his homework. We might expect the father to say "With a good education you can grow up to be anything you want to be", but the cartoonist changes "you want" to "I want". The message is that some parents want to control their children's future careers and lives. It's funny, but is it really true? I don't think so. Of course, there are some parents who try to control their children's futures, but in my experience the majority of parents are happy to let their children choose their own careers. Parents often offer advice, and hope that their children will be successful, but these days the idea that parents can decide their children's futures seems very old-fashioned.

7 Writing: A speech

Lösungsvorschlag:
Across the European Union the average unemployment rate in January 2012 was 10.1%. But for people under 25, it was 22.4%. The highest rate of youth unemployment is in Spain where nearly half the under-25s are out of work. This is very bad news. Firstly, it's expensive. Youth unemployment costs the EU around ?2 billion per week. Secondly, the effects of unemployment on young people can be very serious. How can they start their adult lives if they're not earning a salary? What does it feel like if you're in your mid-20s, and you've never had a job? Governments should spend more money on solving this problem. For example, in my city there's quite a lot of rubbish and not many flowers in the park. The local council could pay some unemployed young people to pick up the rubbish and plant more flowers. That's not a fantastic job, but it would be better than nothing.

8 Speaking: A discussion

Part 1: Interview
Individuelle Lösung

Part 2: Individual long turn
Lösungsvorschlag:

Student A
The first photo shows four teenagers who seem to be in an urban environment. They're wearing fashionable clothes, and all of them are looking at the screens of mobile phones. The photo gives the impression that socializing is an important part of their lives. It also suggests that electronic communication sometimes

Green Line Oberstufe Klasse 10
ISBN: 978-3-12-560021-8

takes the place of real face-to-face communication, because these people are all looking at their phones rather than talking to each other.

Student B
The second photo shows a boy of about the same age as the people in the first photo. He seems to be selling hats at a railway station, and the setting appears to be a developing country in Asia. The photo suggests that the boy is poor, and that his life is mostly about working rather than socializing with his friends.

Part 3: Discussion
Lösungsvorschlag:

Student A
- Teenagers in developed countries aren't necessarily happy.
- Pressures of life, studying and hoping to find a job.
- Money and consumer culture doesn't make people happy.
- The hat-seller may enjoy his work.
- Young people in developing countries may have stronger family and community relationships.
- 'You don't miss what you've never had.'

Student B
- The hat-seller probably works very long hours and earns very little money.
- Earning enough money to live will be a constant problem.
- Problems with health care – what if he becomes ill?
- Less education, fewer opportunities – he may be a hat-seller all his life.
- Mobile phones may not make people happier than face-to-face communication, but the hat-seller has neither. Most of the time he probably works alone.
- Many people in developing countries are aware of how much easier life is in developed countries, and know what they are missing.

9 Speaking: A discussion

Part 1: Interview
Individuelle Lösung

Part 2: Individual long turn
Lösungsvorschlag:

Student A
The first photo shows three teenagers with unconventional hairstyles. All three seem to be dressed in Goth fashion. Perhaps the girl on the left is smiling a little, but the other two look very serious. I can imagine this photo was taken in a shopping centre, or some other place in a city.
The second photo shows a girl who is also wearing Goth clothes sitting on a sofa. The two adults with her are probably her parents. The girl looks angry or upset about something, and the parents seem to be arguing. Perhaps they're arguing about their daughter's choice of clothes. It seems quite a sad picture.

Student B
The third photo shows some young people sitting on the grass. They're all wearing very normal informal clothes. Perhaps they're university students. They seem to be happy, and to be having a very interesting conversation. The fourth photo seems to be a happy family. There is some delicious-looking food on the table, the mother is serving some salad and they are just about to enjoy a meal together. It looks like a fantasy rather than a real situation. I think this photo was probably posed, and the people may be models rather than a genuine family. It seems more like a photo from an advertisement rather than something from real life.

Part 3: Discussion
Lösungsvorschlag:

Student A
- Fashion serves no real purpose and is a waste of time.
- It can cause problems for young people looking for places in higher education and good jobs.
- It creates pointless disagreements with parents.
- It doesn't look good.
- There are more important things to think about than fashion.
- If fashion is so good, why does it keep changing?

Student B
- Fashionable clothes are a form of self-expression.
- It doesn't cost any more than wearing 'normal' clothes.
- A distinct style helps people to find friends with similar interests and opinions.
- It looks good, and makes life a little more interesting for everybody.
- It's connected with popular music and art.

10 Mediation: A summary

Lösungsvorschlag:
Dem Artikel zu Folge bekommen Jugendliche zu wenig Schlaf. Davon bräuchten sie jede Nacht zwischen neun und neuneinhalb Stunden. Zeitiger ins Bett zu gehen, löst das Problem nicht, weil die innerliche Uhr von Jugendlichen anders tickt als die von Erwachsenen. Uns Jugendlichen fällt es schwerer abends einzuschlafen und deshalb kommen wir früh auch nicht so gut aus dem Bett. Es ist erwiesen, dass die meisten Jugendlichen nicht annähernd genug Schlaf bekommen. Das kann sich negativ auf ihre Gesundheit und schulischen Leistungen auswirken. Außerdem verursacht zu wenig Schlaf Gedächtnisprobleme und Lern- / Konzentrationsschwierigkeiten. Zu wenig Schlaf kann krank machen. In dem Artikel steht, dass Jugendliche krank werden können und die schulischen Leistungen beeinträchtigt werden, wenn sie den verpassten Schlaf nicht am Wochenende nachholen können. Hier steht noch etwas Interessantes: wenn Jugendliche zu viel um die Ohren haben, sollte es ihnen erlaubt sein, einige Dinge liegen zu lassen / nicht zu machen. Wenn sie zu viele Hausaufgaben aufbekommen, sollten sich die Eltern an die Schule wenden und darum bitten die Hausaufgaben zu reduzieren.

Green Line Oberstufe Klasse 10
ISBN: 978-3-12-560021-8

11 Mediation: Exchanging information

Lösungsvorschlag:

1 Sie glaubt, dass Mobbing kein wirkliches Problem ist. An ihrer Schule ist es kein Thema.
2 That's unlikely. In most countries, about 90% of students who are asked say that there's bullying in their schools.
3 Sie geht auf eine Mädchenschule und glaubt, dass es vor allem ein Problem unter Jungs ist.
4 Research shows bullying occurs more or less equally among both boys and girls.
5 Sie hat nie erlebt, dass sich die Mädchen an ihrer Schule prügeln.
6 Physical violence isn't the only form of bullying. There are different kinds: verbal attacks, such as calling people names or making fun of them, social isolation by excluding people from a group, saying bad things about people, that kind of thing.
7 Sie sagt, dass das an ihrer Schule auch vorkommt.
8 He says there's cyber-bullying too – using the Internet and text messages for bullying. Have you ever sent somebody a nasty text message?
9 Ja, das hat sie. Aber sie fragt, ob dass nicht nur eine Phase ist, die manche Kinder durchlaufen und die bald vorbei ist.
10 There are more than enough horrible people in the world. How do you think most of them started? Everybody must understand that bullying is not normal, either at school or anywhere else.
11 Macht Petzen es nicht noch schlimmer für Betroffene?
12 No – every school that has started an anti- bullying campaign has reduced it a lot. Schools need to have a culture where bullying is socially unacceptable and will be punished. Victims must turn to their teachers for help or nothing will change, either for them or for future students.
13 Sie sagt, sie hat das Problem verstanden.

Topic 2 Multi-ethnic Britain

1 Listening: Latin Americans in London

Either:
1. a; 2. b; 3. c; 4. b; 5. b; 6. a; 7. b; 8. b

Or:
1. G; 2. F; 3. B; 4. H; 5. A; 6. E; 7. C; 8. D

Tapescript:
Diesen Text finden Sie auf der CD-ROM.

2 Listening: Multiculturalism in the UK

Either:
1. true; 2. false (They met in London.); 3. true; 4. true; 5. false (He thinks he's a mixture of both cultures.); 6. false (They left because of the political situation.); 7. false (She thinks they are very different.); 8. false (Homosexuality isn't tolerated in Iran.); 9. true; 10. true

Or:
1. In the 1970s; 2. West London; 3. Cantonese and English; 4. Chinese New Year; 5. He's a doctor; 6. She didn't speak English very well. 7. At dinner.

Tapescript:
Diesen Text finden Sie auf der CD-ROM.

3 Reading: Illegal immigrants

Either:
1. true; 2. false (Tomu says: '… that was the last time I saw my mother.'); 3. false ('I … joined the others as they climbed into the lorry …'); 4. false (The journey was very long.); 5. not in the text; 6. true; 7. not in the text; 8. true; 9. not in the text; 10. true

Or:
1. … pitch-black / smelt of rubber and something unidentifiable / full of tyres and people.
2. … it would make it harder to detect $CO2$.
3. … inside a big (tractor) tyre.
4. … that someone would come to interview him.
5. … was very different to the ones he had heard at school.
6. … of the fighting there.

Analysis:
1. The text is a dramatized story with autobiographical details, i.e. direct speech and descriptions of people and events make the story interesting.
2. The text might come from a novel.
3. The author could be an illegal immigrant to the UK writing about his own experiences.
4. The purpose of the text could be to inform people about the terrible conditions facing illegal immigrants and to raise awareness of the problems and dangers they are faced with.

Green Line Oberstufe Klasse 10
ISBN: 978-3-12-560021-8

4 Reading: British-born Chinese

Either:
Paragraph 1:
Could you tell us about your origins?
Paragraph 2:
What do you think life was like for your parents when they first moved to the UK?
Paragraph 3:
What was your childhood like?
Paragraph 4:
Do you share the same characteristics as your parents or are there differences?
Paragraph 5:
When you were growing up, did you feel more British or more Chinese?
Paragraph 6:
What areas of Chinese and British culture do you like?
(Have you experienced racism in the UK? – doesn't fit.)

Or:
1. true, line 4; 2. false (Only the father could speak English before they came to the UK.), line 10 – 12; 3. false (The mother is very out-going and talkative.), line 13; 4. true, line 16; 5. false (The writer's earliest memory is going to primary school in London.), line 21; 6. true, line 23; 7. true, line 28; 8. true, line 34; 9. true, line 35; 10. true, line 35

Analysis:
1. The *Illegal immigrants* text was dramatized, i.e. direct speech and descriptions of people and events made the story interesting for the reader. This text is a more straightforward autobiography.
2. The author could be either the son or the daughter of Chinese immigrants to the UK. He / She had is well-educated, speaks fluent English and can speak Mandarin Chinese. Although he / she is proud of his / her Chinese background, he / she feels British.
3. Basically, the author is writing about herself. She uses the historical information about her parents to explain her own background and childhood. The text gives an insight into the feelings of an ethnic Chinese growing up in a British society and trying to find their balance between different cultures.

5 Understanding films: Leicester – a multi-ethnic city

Either:
1. R; 2. H; 3. P; 4. P: 5. R; 6. R

Or:
The film clip is about population changes in places like Leicester and Birmingham, where a majority of residents now has an Asian or a black background. This has caused cultural changes and created an interesting and successful social mix. Hence diversity is seen as being positive.

Analysis:
1. The film is a short clip from the news.
2. It's set in two places. The first is in a classroom in a school called Rushey Mead. The second is set in the streets of Leicester.
3. We hear the voice of the reporter. Then the head teacher of the school talks about why ethnic diversity in schools is a positive thing. The next person is a white woman who also believes that mixed communities are interesting. Then we meet a woman of mixed-race who says that she used to be bullied by white children when she was younger, but she says that the situation has improved a lot. The journalist then sums up the situation.
4. The main purpose of the film is to report on how the ethnic make-up of schools in the UK has changed significantly.
5. The film clip shows mostly images of black and Asian students. The reporter and one of the people who are interviewed are of mixed ethnicity. The street scenes (food, shops, signs) also underline the multicultural flavour of the area.

Transcript:
Diesen Text finden Sie auf der CD-ROM.

6 Writing: A letter to the editor

Lösungsvorschlag:
Dear Editor,
I am writing about a recent cartoon published in your magazine, in which a stereotypical white middle-class, middle-aged couple are discussing what they are going to have for dinner.
The cartoonist appears to convey an ironic mixed-message. The woman offers to cook Mexican, Chinese, or Italian food, and yet she states that if immigrants ('they') want to live in this country, then they should follow the culture of that country. This is ironic because she talks about different types of food, and if immigrants did as she said i.e. follow the culture, then they would only eat the food of that country and not their own culture's food.
I believe that there are people like this in Germany, too. They believe that immigrants should adopt German culture, but they also appreciate being able to choose different ethnic foods from different cultures, and so they send out mixed-messages.
Yours faithfully,
...

7 Writing: A report

Lösungsvorschlag:
The graph compares the percentage of ethnic minority pupils in UK schools in 1999 and in 2009. The graph shows that the number of ethnic minority pupils has risen yearly in every part of the UK. In the north-east and the south-west of England the number has doubled. Inner London remained the place with the highest percentage of ethnic minority pupils in the UK; in 2009 this rose to almost 70%. In Outer London, from 1999 to 2009 the amount increased by almost 10%.

ISBN: 978-3-12-560021-8

I think that the increase is because of the first and second generation immigrant families having children and these children are now entering UK schools. In Germany there are large ethnic communities in big cities such as Berlin, Munich, Dortmund, etc. In some parts of these cities the situation is similar to the UK where a majority of the population have an immigrant backround.

8 Speaking: Cultural tolerance

Part 1: Interview
Lösungsvorschlag:

1. The photo shows an advert somewhere in Britain. The advert is for H&M. I think they are advertising bikinis.
2. Someone has painted over the advert with black paint.
3. I think someone felt offended by the picture of woman in bikini.

Part 2: Individual long turn
Lösungsvorschlag:

Student A
A lot of both Muslims and non-Muslims in Germany would like Germany to be more sensitive to Islamic culture. So, for example, we should avoid cartoons of Muslims which are provocative and deliberately offensive.
I can agree with that. But I don't agree with people who want to ban adverts of women in bikinis in areas where Muslims live. Do we also ban adverts for beer in such areas? Cultural tolerance must work both ways.

Student B
Our constitution allows everyone to practise their own religion, but only as long as this conforms with our laws. For example, we don't allow a man to have more than one wife. A few extremists demand Shariah law, but I think that the majority of Muslims living here understand that Germany isn't an Islamic country and they respect our liberal traditions and laws. Most Muslims don't have a problem with this because they come from countries that also have a long history of cultural tolerance. However, civil law and cultural traditions do sometimes clash. For example, when a German court declared that ritual circumcision was child abuse and made it illegal. Both Jewish and Muslim communities protested.

Part 3: Discussion
Lösungsvorschlag:

Student A
People should follow the traditions of the country they live in. The hajib is acceptable in western societies, but many non-Muslims find the burqa offensive and degrading for women. In western culture it isn't good to hide your face because people can't see what you're thinking, or who is under the veil.

Student B
In our society people have the freedom to practise their religion; they should also be free to wear whatever they want – even something as extreme as a burqa. If a Muslim woman wants to hide herself in a burqa, then she should have the freedom to do so.

9 Speaking: Cultural heritage

Part 1: Interview
Lösungsvorschlag:

1. They look like they might be high-school students. They're obviously of mixed ethnicity. The mood is warm and friendly.
2. They've probably just done something together which they enjoyed. Perhaps they've just had an important exam or it's the end of term.
3. Photo 2 looks as if it has been taken at a white, middle-class school where there are few or even no ethnic minorities. Perhaps a public school? In contrast to photo 1 the situation is formal. The pupils are looking at something in front of them. They're subdued and there is no interaction between them.
4. Placing these photos together invites us to contrast them. Photo 1 is multiethnic, photo 2 isn't. Photo 1 is very relaxed and informal, warm, friendly and colourful – photo 2 is its antithesis. (The message is that multiethnic societies are better, happier and friendlier than monoethnic societies.)

Part 2: Individual long turn
Lösungsvorschlag:

Student A
Photo 1 shows a group of young people, photo 2 is a close-up and shows only four faces clearly. So photo 1 emphasizes the group and photo 2 the individual. The students in photo 1 are of mixed gender and mixed ethnicity, but the pupils in photo 2 are all white. In photo 1 the pupils wear normal clothing, the pupils in photo 2 are wearing a school uniform. The students in photo 1 are enjoying themselves, those in photo 2 aren't.

Student B
In photo 1 the students are multi-ethnic and they look very happy, but in the second photo, the students are all white and they look quite serious. They look like they are in a lesson. The happy smiling faces and bright clothes of the boys and girls in photo 1 makes a sharp contrast to the school uniforms and serious expressions of the pupils in photo 2. I think the message is: Multiculturalism is fun!

Part 3: Role-play
Lösungsvorschlag:

A: My name is Sumitra and I'm the girl with glasses on the left of the photo. My grandparents were from India, but my parents and I were all born here, and I've lived here all my life.
B: My name is Roberto and I'm the good-looking boy behind Sumitra. I was born in Colombia, but my parents brought me here when I was just a baby.

Green Line Oberstufe Klasse 10
ISBN: 978-3-12-560021-8

A: I've never been to India. I'd like to go there, but only for a holiday. I wouldn't want to live there.
B: It's the same for me. I'm not Colombian. My parents are different because they still have emotional ties to the old country. At home we speak Spanish and my parents' English still isn't very good.
A: I've never had that problem. Even my grandparents spoke English. It annoys me when friends who should know better ask me if I speak Hindi at home and have curry for breakfast.
B: They're just curious and that's not a bad thing. I get asked some weird questions too. My favourite is: Do we all chew coca leaves in the evening? Or when girls ask me if I can dance the rumba!
A: Oh, I love Latin American dance music. Don't you?
B: No, not really. What I really like is Britasia music.
A: Me too. What's your favourite food?
B: Tandoori chicken. And yours?
A: Vegetable lasagne.

10 Mediation: A summary

Lösungsvorschlag:
Derzeit leben über eine halbe Million Araber im Vereinigten Königreich; die meisten von ihnen in London. Sie haben ihre Wurzeln in Ägypten, Marokko, Palästina, im Jemen oder Libanon. Andere kamen aus den Golfstaaten oder dem Irak ins Vereinigte Königreich. Letztere gründeten mit den Einnahmen aus Ölgeschäften Unternehmen in London.
Mitte des 19. Jahrhunderts ließen sich jemenitische Seeleute entlang der Themse nieder. In den 1930er Jahren wanderten viele Iraker ins Land ein, um in London zu leben und zu arbeiten. In den 1940er und 1960er Jahren folgte eine Einwanderungswelle aus Ägypten. Die Einwanderung nahm in den 1950er und 1960er Jahren zu, als sich die arabische Welt vom Kolonialismus befreite und eigenständiger wurde. Eine nächste Zuwanderungswelle folgte in den 1970er Jahren aus dem Libanon, das sich damals im Kriegszustand befand.
Die Kultur der arabischen Welt zeigt sich auf vielfältige Art und Weise überall in London: libanesische Kebab-Stuben, Shisha-Bars, marokkanische Restaurants, aber auch in der Kleidung. Viele Araber wohnen im Zentrum von London, vor allem um die Edgeware Road. Viele Araber wohnen aber auch in den teuersten Wohngegenden von Westminster und Knightsbridge.

11 Mediation: Chinese New Year

You:
(1) When is Chinese New Year and how is it celebrated?
(2) 2013 findet das chinesische Neujahrsfest am 10. Februar statt. Auf dem Trafalgar Square gibt es ein großes Fest, wo traditionelle Tänze aufgeführt werden. Außerdem gibt es ein Feuerwerk, Musik, und natürlich eine Menge zu essen!
(3) What's the animal symbol for 2013?
(4) Es ist das Jahr der Schlange, das heißt dass in ihrem Haus niemand Hunger leiden wird. Es wird ein gutes Jahr für Geschäftesabschlüsse, aber ein schlechtes für Umzüge oder Hochzeiten.
(5) My brother was born in the Year of the Monkey – what are his characteristics?
(6) Er sagt, dass Affen als intelligent und gesprächig gelten, aber sie langweilen sich schnell. Er fragt, ob das zu dir passt.
(7) A little bit. Can you tell us more about the New Year celebration?
(8) Die ganze Familie trifft sich zu einem großen gemeinsamen Abendessen. Kinder bekommen Geld in kleinen roten Umschlägen geschenkt.

Topic 3 The Blue Planet

1 Listening: Enough is enough!

Either:
a) 3; b) 6; c) 2; d) 1; e) 5; f) 4

Or:
1. increased; 2. economic; 3. twice; 4. oil; 5. health; 6. noise; 7. houses

Tapescript:
Diesen Text finden Sie auf der CD-ROM.

2 Listening: Green shoppers

Either:
a) 5; b) 4; c) 1; d) 3; e) 6; f) 2

Or:
1. true; 2. false; 3. false; 4. true; 5. true; 6. false; 7. true

Tapescript:
Diesen Text finden Sie auf der CD-ROM.

3 Reading: A poem

Either:
1 responsible 2 environment 3 generations 4 angry 5 disasters 6 behaviour 7 produced 8 choices

Or:
1. No, she doesn't.
2. polluted air, holes in the ozone layer, disappearing ice caps
3. smartphones, cheap clothes, coffee to go
4. They may have been made in a way which damages the environment.
5. They could decide not to support polluting industries by buying their products.

Analysis:
1. a) lines 5 to 9 b) lines 10 to 12 c) lines 13 to 16
2. *Lösungsvorschlag:* I think "not guilty" is a good title because at the beginning of the poem you feel that nothing is your fault if you are a young person. Then later in the poem you see that young people could become guilty of destroying the environment but they

Green Line Oberstufe Klasse 10
ISBN: 978-3-12-560021-8

have the chance not to do that. You really want to stay "not guilty".

3. a) Can nobody stop it? Does nobody hear?
   b) If their products are cheap, how much should we ask
   About how they were made, who was given the task?
   How were they all made, do we want to know?
   Will we allow this disaster to be our fault, too?
   c) Did I build the factories that darken the sky?

4 Reading: Amazon

Either:

Tribe	Amazon
- three in the team - stayed in one community - immersed in one culture	- six in the team - constantly moving - talking to different groups of people

Or:
1. false ("... after a few month's break at home.");
2. true; 3. false; 4. true; 5. not in the text; 6. true;
7. true; 8. true; 9. false ("So I'm up for taking anything that can help.")

Analysis:
1. The main purpose of the text is to give the reader background to the making of a new documentary series and to explain how the new documentary, *Amazon*, is different from the last one, *Tribe*. The writer talks about his feelings before filming starts and on the first day of filming.
2. The writer uses the form of a diary, mainly in the present tense describing things as they happen. The reader can feel as if he / she is with the team as they wait for their flight and share the feelings of the writer. Also, on the first day of filming, the writer can share the feelings of the team as they happen.
   At the airport, the reader can learn the background to the making of the documentary by sharing the writer's thoughts about what the team are going to try and do. In Mismi, the writer can contrast descriptions of the landscape and the river source with the illness – altitude sickness – the team are suffering from.
3. The writer uses the words *barren, lunar, parched, dusty, brown, grey* to describe the landscape. We get the feeling that it is completely dry, no water, nothing grows there. In contrast, the words used to describe the river source are: *water, pours, spurts, cold crystal liquid gush, spring*. We get the feeling of water everywhere, moving fast, feeling fresh. He also uses the words *inspiring, elemental, mysterious* to show the power he feels when he sees the river source.

5 Understanding films: Deforestation and global warming

Either:
1. for farming, for wood 2. furniture, paper, construction 3. a few decades 4. 1 to 6 degrees Celsius (Centigrade) 5. Trees help the earth to breathe by producing oxygen and removing carbon dioxide from the atmosphere and storing it.

Or:
Lösungsvorschlag:
Rising levels of carbon-dioxide lead to the greenhouse effect. When sunbeams hit the earth, some of the heat is absorbed by greenhouse gases. Human activity produces more greenhouse gases. These gases become thicker and stop heat escaping into space. The result is global warming, which can make ice melt and sea levels rise. Coastal regions can flood. Salt content decreases and species die out.

Analysis:
1. The images make the viewer feel worried and upset about what we are doing to the rainforests and the cost to the planet.
2. The music is sad and depressing. It tells us that the information in the film is bad news.

Transcript:
Diesen Text finden Sie auf der CD-ROM.

6 Writing: A letter to the editor

Lösungsvorschlag:
- To bury your head in the sand means to refuse to face a problem.
- The cartoonists has used irony by showing a person refusing to face the serious problem of global warming (which creates more deserts) by burying his head in the desert sand.
- The letter could contain some of the following ideas: We bury our heads in the sand because we know we should recycle rubbish / walk or cycle instead of driving / avoid flying / reduce our energy usage at home / use less paper and plastic etc. but it's easier to ignore the problem. The consequences are global warming / pollution / more deserts / more floods / natural resources running out.

7 Writing: A speech

To prepare:
- The young woman believes that it is a waste of time to help just a few toads when all the others will die. The old man believes that if he can help a few toads to live, he has done something very important.
- The toad is a metaphor for any individual action we can take to help the environment, e.g. recycling one bottle.

Green Line Oberstufe Klasse 10
ISBN: 978-3-12-560021-8

Lösungsvorschlag:
- Every individual action is important.
- We could each do the following: recycle paper, plastic, glass every time we use it / switch off lights / walk or cycle instead of driving / buy green products / have holidays at home instead of flying abroad.
- If we all did these things, we could reduce pollution / save energy / encourage companies to produce more green products / reduce global warming / save natural resources.
- It is true that one person can't change the world, but we can all do something and together make a big difference.

8 Speaking: The environment

Part 1: Interview
Individuelle Lösung

Part 2: Individual long turn
Lösungsvorschlag:

Cartoon 1 shows an overheated world. Carbon dioxide emissions from factories and cars and the use of chemicals on farms lead to the greenhouse effect where the world gets hotter and hotter. Deforestation releases carbon dioxide into the atmosphere and is one of the causes of global warming which causes the ice caps to melt and sea levels to rise. Species die out as the salt content of the sea decreases. Coastal regions are flooded and there are more deserts where nothing can grow.

Cartoon 2 shows the effects of air pollution caused by the smoke and fumes from cars and factories. People find it hard to breathe and get illnesses like asthma. Chemicals in the air cause acid rain which hurts animals and plants.

Part 3: Discussion
Individuelle Lösung

9 Speaking: Energy and tourism

Part 1: Interview
Individuelle Lösung

Part 2: Individual long turn
Lösungsvorschlag:

Student A
We waste energy at home by … leaving lights on / switching on washing machines and dishwashers before they are full / leaving taps on/ having a bath instead of a shower / turning on the heating instead of putting on more clothes / leaving televisions and computers on standby / using the car instead of walking or car-sharing or cycling / over-lighting our houses at Christmas (as in picture).

Student B
We're using too much fossil fuel (coal, oil, natural gas) for energy. Fossil fuels are running out so we need to find other energy sources that won't run out. Sunlight (solar energy) can be used to heat and light homes, to generate electricity, to heat hot water. People can put solar panels on their homes (as in the picture). This is becoming more and more popular. Wind and water can also be used to make energy, e.g. windmills and hydroelectric power.

Part 3: Discussion
Individuelle Lösung

10 Mediation: A leaflet

Lösungsvorschlag:
1. Indem du den Computer ganz ausschaltest, kannst du Strom und Geld sparen.
2. Jedes Jahr werden Millionen Tonnen an Papier einfach weggeworfen. Man kann den Drucker auf ‚beidseitig drucken' einstellen, um Papier zu sparen und Papier, das man nicht mehr braucht in die Papiertonne
werfen / zum Recyclinghof bringen.
3. Einmal pro Woche sollte man sich vegetarisch ernähren. Da Tiere viel Wasser und Lebensraum brauchen, schont man so die Natur.
4. Fast 90% aller Plastikflaschen werden nicht recycelt und brauchen Jahrtausende, um zu verrotten. In Mehrzweckbehältern kann man Leitungswasser abfüllen, was der Umwelt zugute kommt und Geld spart.
5. Duschen ist besser als Baden (braucht doppelt so viel Wasser). So kann man Wasser und Strom / Gas sparen. Letzteres wird zum Erhitzen benötigt.
6. Um den Müll zu reduzieren, kann man Sachen in einen Second-Hand-Laden bringen oder dort kaufen.
7. Man sollte das Licht ausschalten, wenn man den Raum verlässt, da sich der Raum sonst durch die Wärme der Glühbirne aufheizt und klimatisiert / heruntergekühlt werden muss.
8. Aus gebrauchten Geschenktüten, Schleifen, Geschenkpapier, Stadtplänen, Stoff oder Zeitungen kann man Geschenkpapier selbst herstellen.

11 Mediation: Voluntary service

Lösungsvorschlag:
1. Anna fragt, wo sie arbeiten könnte. In welchen Ländern werden Freiwillige gebraucht?
2. There are lots of countries where you can work. For example, an important new project will be starting soon in Costa Rica.
3. Costa Rica würde sie interessieren. Was für ein Projekt ist das dort?
4. It's an animal-care project based at an Animal Rescue Centre in the south of the country. The idea is to help sick animals get strong again and release them back into the wild. The volunteers at the centre find animals that have been hurt, for example in road accidents. When they're better they're taken back to their natural habitat.
5. Und was wäre ihre Aufgabe?
6. Tom says that your job would be to care for the animals until they can be returned to the wild. You'd feed the animals, collect data, give presentations to schoolchildren and explain the importance of wild animals and plants. Education is really the most

Green Line Oberstufe Klasse 10
ISBN: 978-3-12-560021-8

important part of the job and there is also a weekly environmental awareness programme on local radio, and you would take part in this by talking to local people about their problems.

7. Das würde ihr gefallen. Was muss sie als nächstes tun?
8. Tom says that there are a few introductory training weekends coming up this summer. You could come along and find out more and meet some like-minded people! If you give him your e-mail address, he'll send you more information and an application form.

Topic 4 South Africa

1 Listening: Visiting Robben Island

Either:
1. true; 2. false; 3. false; 4. true; 5. true; 6. false; 7. false; 8. true

Or:
1. her mother 2. reading a guide book 3. Mandela's time on Robben Island 4. Mandela's generosity and dignity 5. visiting the island / watching the film again 6. a warm jacket

Tapescript:
Diesen Text finden Sie auf der CD-ROM.

2 Listening: The history of Robben Island

Either:
1. a, b; 2. b; 3. c; 4. b

Or:
Reihenfolge: 1 D; 2A; 3 B; 4 F; 5 E; 6 C

Tapescript:
Diesen Text finden Sie auf der CD-ROM.

3 Reading: Storytelling in Africa

Either:
2. soft and fast; 3. fast; 4. slow and soft; 5. loud; 6. fast and loud

Or:
Lösungsvorschlag:
1. … that it's OK to laugh with them and laugh at the silly mouse; 2. … nothing bad happens to the mouse, it's a harmless joke; 3. … it highlights the important parts of the story; 4. … stop when the audience laughs and laugh with them and then go on with the story.

Analysis:
Possible arguments: knowledge gives the hyena a better insight into the way the world works and so it has the power to use the information for its own interests. With its superior knowledge it creates a situation where the mouse feels confused and afraid and this fear gives the hyena power over the mouse. The story shows that knowledge can be used to exploit and to bully others.

4 Reading: Mama Africa

Either:
1. 1957 top of the charts in South Africa, 1959 move to the USA, recordings with Harry Belafonte, performed with Paul Simon, 1974 performance in Zaire, parts in15 films, Free Nelson Mandela concert 1988, 1990 first concert in South Africa after 30 years in exile
2. demand for human rights for all South Africans, loss of passport in 1960, represented Guinea at the United Nations, Dag Hammarskjöld Peace Prize 1986, Free Mandela concert 1988, 2001 Otto Hahn Peace Medal,

Green Line Oberstufe Klasse 10
ISBN: 978-3-12-560021-8

Or:
1. true; 2. true; 3. false (She was invited to sing in the USA.); 4. true; 5. not in text; 6. not in text; 7. true

Analysis:
The author uses the life of Makeba as an example of the way the Apartheid government hurt the black people of South Africa. For example, black people had no freedom of speech. When Makeba spoke about human rights in the USA they punished her by taking away her passport so that she couldn't return home. Like many other black South Africans she was in exile for many years.

5 Understanding films: Cape Town, South Africa

a) 1. Table Mountain; 2. The Portuguese; 3. Vasco da Gama; 4. The Dutch; 5. The Dutch East India company's garden

b) Still 1: Shows the back of the climber, the camera is lower than the person, the cinematic point of view is from the bottom, looking up.
Still 2: Shows the opposite cinematic point of view to Still 1. The camera is looking down on the climber.
Still 3: A long shot, showing Cape Town from a distance with Table Mountain large in the background.
Still 4: The camera is looking down from the top of the mountain onto the climber, with the sea down below in the background.
The many changes in perspective make Table Mountain seem very high.

Transcript:
Diesen Text finden Sie auf der CD-ROM.

6 Writing: Poverty in South Africa

Lösungsansätze:
– natural abilities, e.g. mechanical aptitude
– keen to learn
– educational, health, training programmes

7 Writing: The breadline

Lösungsansätze:
– poverty, starvation, desperation
– high prices, unfair, out of reach

8 Speaking: Piercings

Part 1: Interview
Individuelle Lösungen

Part 2: Individual long turn

Student A
teenage girls, wear ear plugs, holes in ears, look happy

Student B
African girl: beadwork, size of ear plugs and holes in ears
European girl: European style of piercing, nose and tongue piercings, smaller piercings

Part 3: Role-play
Individuelle Lösungen

9 Speaking: An unusual house

Part 1: Interview
Individuelle Lösungen

Part 2: Individual long turn
Lösungsvorschlag:

The house is built of stone and in the form of a boot. The tip of the shoe and its back are painted white, but the rest of the shoe is built from bricks. The house has got several windows, a door and a roof. It also has lacing and you can see the sole and the heel. Maybe an artist lives in the shoe house because it has such an unusual shape. I think it would be fun to live in a house with such a shape.

Part 3: Role-play
Individuelle Lösungen

10 Mediation: The big prize!

Lösungsvorschlag:
1. The writer won a trip to South Africa and is waiting at Frankfurt Airport for the rest of her group.
2. The trip to South Africa was long, but the South African Airways crew was very good. The group spent the first day in Soweto and then travelled on to Port Elizabeth.
3. They were picked up at the airport in Port Elizabeth and after a 90-minute journey they arrived at the Amakhala Game Reserve. The game rangers were waiting for them and their luggage was reloaded onto jeeps. On their way to the lodge they saw an elephant, zebras, ostriches and antelopes.
4. Two days of safari, getting up early at 6 a.m. There was a lot of time to observe animals and take photos.
5. David, the ranger, took the group close to a family of lions. There was a mother with five cubs. The writer was delighted with the experience and could have stayed for hours.
6. The day was spent at the craft market and the writer bought a lot of key rings made by locals as gifts to take home. She enjoyed seeing a bit of everyday life in South Africa. She also loved the great meals they served at the lodge every day.

11 Mediation: A conversation

1. I liked the elephants the best, even if they were tame. The size of the animals is impressive. I'd love to go on an elephant safari.
2. There was a lot of variety in the programme. Time passed very quickly indeed.
3. The tent camp was really cool. It's a good idea to have wooden floors and insect netting in the tents. The cupboard with a lock is a must. It's OK to have 4 beds in a tent, but only when everybody gets on well together. Perhaps two-man tents are also needed?

Green Line Oberstufe Klasse 10
ISBN: 978-3-12-560021-8

4. I think three toilets and two showers aren't enough for a camp of this size. You need at least four of each. It was great to have hot water from the solar heating system.
5. Parents will feel better if they know there's an electric fence around the camp and night guards with guns. They should also know that the elephants are tame and the rangers are well-qualified. And that the water is from a bore hole and safe to drink.

Topic 5 Make a difference

1 Listening Fundraising

Either:
1. a children's ward / hospital; 2. nearly £1,000; 3. about £2,000; 4. It's bigger. / It has more members.; 5. a fun-run; 6. on the Internet; 7. club doesn't have much money; 8. bring people together / feel part of a group; 9. newspapers, TV, Internet (Facebook / website); 10. think about it more

Or:
1. can't cook; 2. it's unhealthy; 3. too expensive / not everybody can take part; 4. easy to organize; 5. parents would disapprove; 6. beard

Tapescript:
Diesen Text finden Sie auf der CD-ROM.

2 Listening: Adam's story

Either:
1. c; 2. a; 3. b; 4. a; 5. c; 6 . c

Or:
1. A lawyer. 2. He was robbed. 3. A good education, a supportive family, a place to live. 4. Next to a church. 5. A children's playground. 6. Three years. 7. Homeless people and volunteers with homes. 8. Everyone.

Tapescript:
Diesen Text finden Sie auf der CD-ROM.

3 Reading: Fixing a hole

Either:
1. true; 2. true; 3. not in the text; 4. false (The flowers came from his window box); 5. not in the text; 6. true; 7. false (Only on local TV); 8. true

Or:
1. b; 2. c; 3. a; 4. c; 5. b; 6. a; 7. b

Analysis
1. He isn't politically active.
2. Here 'guerilla gardening' is described as planting flowers and other plants on building sites or land belonging to a factory.
3. Some neighbours laugh at John. Most of them ignore at first, but then they start helping him. They turn his initiative into a community project.
4. Although shy and not having much confidence, he makes a positive impression on the people he meets: his neighbours, the television interviewer, his new colleagues.
5. The story is written in the first person, with the narrator making jokes about himself and his relationship with others: 'Laugh? I almost did', 'at least I think I think it's great'. The narrator mostly uses a simple conversational style, with lots of phrases

Green Line Oberstufe Klasse 10
ISBN: 978-3-12-560021-8

which are mostly used in spoken English: 'to be honest', 'it's no big deal'. This adds to the humorous tone of the story.

6. It seems to be a poor, inner-city area with a high level of unemployment. It suffers from vandalism: *'One Saturday night some kids destroyed most of the gardens.* However, there seems to be a sense of community of some kind.
7. 'Fixing a hole' can also be interpreted as 'solving a problem'. Not only are dangerous potholes turned into attractive mini-gardens, but this project has filled some of the holes in John's life, since it has brought him a new job, new friends and a potential girlfriend. The project has also repaired the local neighbourhood by giving it a sense of community.

4 Reading: Protesters win a battle against development

Either:
1. c; 2. b; 3. a; 4. c; 5. a; 6. c

Or:
1. true; 2. true; 3. not in text; 4. false (There are 400 adult bitterns in the whole UK.); 5. not in text (We only know that he takes photographs); 6. false (The animals need the area around the reserve to find food.); 7. false (She feels that people can make a difference.); 8. true; 9. false (The council still wants to build somewhere.)

Analysis:
1. No, it supports the protestors. It only interviews people who are pleased about the decision.
2. The style of writing is factual with quotations from the people who were interviewed. This text could be found in a local newspaper or on a news website.
3. Harry was 'amazed' at the building plans. Jane says she was 'furious' and would have 'felt angry about this forever' but now she feels 'proud to have been part of the campaign'. Sheila says she is 'delighted' about the decision.
4. He thinks that if the council were allowed to build on a nature reserve, no other place would be safe from development.
5. She thinks that because of the state of the economy the new houses would not be sold.
6. The metaphor compares the protestors' campaign to a war in which there will be other battles.

5 Understanding films: Barefoot College

Either:
1. true; 2. false (It's a meeting for students to discuss their education); 3. true; 4. true; 5. false (most of them are adults); 6. false (There are lots of languages); 7. true; 8. false (Everyone eats together); 9. true; 10. true

Or:
1. He was surprised how much responsibility and respect they were shown. 2. They usually study in the evening after work. 3. They are learning to repair solar-powered lights. This is a useful in villages with little or no electricity. 4. The narrator is saying that the women can repair the solar-powered lights as well as men can. 5. He says that the most important lesson is that all the students are equal. 6. She used to be a student, but is now a teacher / training coordinator in the school. 7. She believes that things will get better when there are more educated people who can make good decisions.

Transcript:
Diesen Text finden Sie auf der CD-ROM.

6 Writing: A post

Lösungsvorschlag:

Your post suggests that we should all just sit at home and wait for somebody else to solve the problems of the world. I absolutely disagree with this idea. Most improvements in society have happened because ordinary people decided to work together to change things. Without that, we would still have slavery, children working in factories and women would be unable to vote. Yes, in many cases only governments have the power to change things, but their job is to listen to the people who elected them. If nobody is calling for change, then there will be no change. Time and time again throughout history ordinary people have united to change the world for the better, and it's our responsibility to continue that tradition.

7 Writing: Children in Bangladesh

Lösungsvorschlag:

The children in this photo are having lessons in a charity school before or after going to their jobs, many of them producing clothes for export to Western countries. This situation is common in developing countries. Instead of studying full time, millions of children are working and studying part time or not at all. This is bad not just for the children themselves, but also for the economies of the countries as a whole, because it keeps the average standard of education lower than it could otherwise be. Should Western companies stop doing business with countries where child labour is common? This is a difficult question to answer. The money earned from this kind of industry is often very important to the economy of the country. Also, in many cases, the family of these children need the money they earn in order to survive. In my opinion Western companies should continue doing business with these countries, but use their influence to improve pay and conditions, and to work towards a future where all children only study until they are at least 16.

8 Speaking: Developing countries

Part 1: Interview
Individuelle Lösungen

Green Line Oberstufe Klasse 10
ISBN: 978-3-12-560021-8

Part 2: Individual long turn
Lösungsvorschlag:

Student A
The photo shows a dentist checking a young person's teeth. The equipment is very basic. A very large number of people are standing around and watching. They could be patients or the relatives of patients. Some of them are holding pieces of paper. These could be records of their treatment. This photo shows that things can be very different in developing countries. It's impossible to imagine conditions like this in a dental clinic in Germany.

Student B
The photo seems to show the inside of a small plane or a helicopter which has been turned into an air ambulance. In developing countries, many people live in villages which are very far from hospitals, or they may not be very far from a hospital but the roads are so bad that the journey takes a very long time. Air ambulances can help in this situation because they can transport people to hospital very quickly.

Part 3: Discussion
Lösungsansatz:

Student A
- Ten months is a long time to spend away from home.
- It will interrupt your education – you'll forget what you've studied.
- It will be hot and uncomfortable.
- You may get sick.
- It could be dangerous. What if there's a war or some natural disaster?

Student B
- It'll be good to help people in need.
- Work like this gives you a different perspective an it builds character.
- I'll learn a lot from doing it.
- Something like this looks good on a CV.
- It's not important to be comfortable all the time.
- It won't be dangerous – the volunteer organisation will look after me.
- Crossing a busy street at home can be just as dangerous.

9 Speaking:

Part 1: Interview
Individuelle Lösungen

Part 2: Individual long turn
Lösungsvorschlag:

Student A
The first cartoon shows a group of people at a demonstration. All the messages one their signs are negative: No! Don't! Never! etc. The joke is that the protestor feels this negative demonstration is positive. The cartoon raises an interesting idea. Preventing, or trying to prevent, something bad from happening is a good thing, and naturally this makes people feel positive about themselves. Even when a demonstration is not successful, it can have a positive effect in bringing people together and in raising awareness of an issue.

Student B
This cartoon contrasts an anti-technology message with the fact that the Internet is now important for organizing a demonstration.
It made me think of anti-capitalism demonstrations, which are organized using computers and mobile phones made by large international companies. The cartoon raises an interesting idea. Do people sometimes protest about things which they are benefiting from and wouldn't want to give up?

Part 3: Discussion
Lösungsansatz:

Student A
- Demonstrations almost never bring about change because politicians don't take any notice of them.
- Sometimes a few protestors resort to violence, and this gives the cause a bad name.
- We elect governments and local authorities, so we should accept their decisions.
- Most demonstrations are about things which are only important to a minority of people.

Student B
- Demonstrations played a part in ending slavery, getting votes for women, ending Apartheid and bringing about many other major changes and reforms.
- If people don't protest, politicians won't necessarily know how unhappy people are about something.
- The majority of demonstrations are peaceful.
- Not everybody voted for the party in power.
- Just because something doesn't affect everybody in a country doesn't mean it's unimportant.

10 Mediation: A summary

Lösungsvorschlag:
Sicherlich hast du schon einmal von Fairtrade-Tee, Kaffee und Schokolade gehört, aber es gibt auch noch andere Dinge, wie Kleidung, Blumen oder Müsli. Dabei geht es nicht nur darum, den Produzenten in Entwicklungsländern einen fairen Preis zu zahlen. Den Landwirten wird ein Mindestabnahmepreis garantiert, auch wenn der Marktpreis darunter liegt. Somit haben sie ein garantiertes Einkommen, das ihnen die Investition in Bildung, Gesundheitswesen und Trinkwasserversorgung ermöglicht. Davon profitieren nicht nur die Landwirte, sondern die ganze Gemeinschaft. Unternehmen, die Arbeitskräfte einstellen, müssen nachweisen, dass die Zusatzeinkünfte, die durch Fairtrade entstehen, den Arbeitskräften zu gute kommen. Außerdem müssen die Unternehmen versprechen, dass die Arbeitsbedingungen sicher sind, keine Diskriminierung am Arbeitsplatz herrscht und keine Kinder beschäftigt werden. Fairtrade hat zu einer positiven Veränderung beigetragen, weil es die Lebensbedingungen vieler Menschen weltweit verbessert hat.

Green Line Oberstufe Klasse 10
ISBN: 978-3-12-560021-8

11 Mediation: Exchanging information

Lösungsvorschlag:

1 Frank is running in a marathon for charity in Barcelona, and he'd like you to sponsor him.
2 Sheila möchte wissen, welcher Organisation die Spenden zu gute kommen.
3 The runners choose their own charities. Frank is raising money for Médecins Sans Frontiers. They send doctors and medical equipment to developing countries, especially places where there are wars.
4 Sie kennt die Organisation, aber sie versteht nicht ganz wie du sie unterstützt, indem du einen Marathon läufst.
5 You agree to give some money, and he agrees to finish the marathon and to pass the money on to the charity.
6 Sheila meint, du musst nach Barcelona fliegen und das Hotel bezahlen. Sie befürchtet, dass du so in erster Linie einen Urlaub finanzierst und quasi nebenher am Marathon teilnimmst.
7 Frank says that he'll pay for the trip himself. He won't fly or stay at a hotel. He'll travel by bus and stay at a camping site outside of the city.
8 Sie fragt, wie viel sie dir geben soll.
9 That's up to you. Every euro helps.
10 Sie würde dir fünf Euro geben.
11 Frank says thank you. It won't be wasted. Médecins Sans Frontiers are an extremely efficient charity. They spend very little on overheads, so almost all the money they get is spent on the actual work.
12 Sie erhöht auf 10 Euro, weil Ärzte ohne Grenzen gute Arbeit leisten und sie es sich leisten kann. Sie fliegt nächste Woche zurück nach Kanada, deshalb will sie dir das Geld gleich geben.
13 Frank says that's very kind of you and thank you.
14 Sie wünscht dir viel Spaß in Barcelona. Sie sagt, sie war vor ein paar Jahren dort. Es ist eine tolle Stadt.

Green Line Oberstufe Klasse 10
ISBN: 978-3-12-560021-8

Lösungen Language in use

Topic 1 Growing up

1 Language in use

1. D; 2. C; 3. D; 4. B; 5. C; 6. D; 7. A; 8. C; 9. B; 10. D

2 Language in use

1. completely; 2. constantly; 3. Obviously; 4. fast; 5. recently; 6. nearly; 7. actually; 8. Frankly; 9. responsibly; 10. Eventually

Topic 2 Multi-ethnic Britain

1 Language in use: Potential dangers

1. wanting; 2. (life-)changing; 3. to speak; 4. to divide; 5. speaking; 6. taking; 7. to influence; 8. choosing; 9. denying; 10. Tolerating

2 Language in use

1. conditions; 2. residents; 3. ethnic; 4. perceived; 5. fail; 6. glare at; 7. abuse; 8. discriminated; 9. mainstream; 10. forced

Topic 3 The Blue Planet

1 Language in use: Smog

1. industrial; 2. powerful; 3. production; 4. poisonous; 5. unaware; 6. pollution; 7. development; 8. effective; 9. renewable; 10. shortage

2 Language in use: Pandas

1. A; 2. B; 3. A; 4. C; 5. A; 6. B; 7. A; 8. B; 9. C; 10. B

Topic 4 South Africa

1 Language in use: South Africa

1. to; 2. from; 3. of; 4. of; 5. with; 6. about; 7. to; 8. of; 9. by; 10. in

2 Language in use: The new South Africa

1. democracy; 2. majority; 3. Apartheid / segregation; 4. liberation; 5. equal

3 Language in use: A better future for all

1. perhaps; 2. could; 3. might; 4. would; 5. should

4 Language in use: Tips for the trip

1. B; 2. B; 3. C; 4. B; 5. A; 6. C; 7. B; 8. C; 9. A; 10. B

Topic 5 Make a difference

1 Language in use:

1. C; 2. B; 3. C; 4. B; 5. B; 6. C; 7. C; 8. D; 9. A; 10. A

2 Language in use

1. are; 2. have 3. in; 4. been; 5. in; 6. on / about; 7. about; 8. to; 9. on; 10. part; 11. raise / collect; 12. make

Green Line Oberstufe Klasse 10
ISBN: 978-3-12-560021-8

Hörverstehenstexte zu den Vorschlägen zur Leistungsmessung

Track	Unit	Text/Übungstitel	Seite	Übung	Spielzeit
1	1	Listening: A book review	3	1	4'19"
2	1	Listening: Summer camp	4	2	3'56"
3	2	Listening: Latin Americans in London	17	1	3'57"
4	2	Listening: Multiculturalism in the UK	18	2	4'08"
5	3	Listening: Enough is enough!	29	1	5'17"
6	3	Listening: Green shoppers	30	2	4'20"
7	4	Listening: Visiting Robben Island	42	1	4'03"
8	4	Listening: The history of Robben Island	43	2	4'26"
9	5	Listening: Fundraising	54	1	4'14"
10	5	Listening: Adam's story	55	2	4'35"

Gesamtspielzeit: 43'12"

Bildquellennachweis

UM1.1 Fotosearch Stock Photography (Image Source), Waukesha, WI; **Um1.2** Avenue Images GmbH (Westend61), Hamburg; **UM4.1** iStockphoto (Anton Gvozdikov), Calgary, Alberta; **4.1** Fotosearch Stock Photography (Image Source), Waukesha, WI; **6.1** Thinkstock (photos.com), München; **11.1** www.CartoonStock.com (Baldwin, Mike), Bath; **12.1** iStockphoto (Izabela Habur), Calgary, Alberta; **12.2** iStockphoto (Niko Guido), Calgary, Alberta; **13.1** iStockphoto (parema), Calgary, Alberta; **13.2** iStockphoto (Lisa F. Young), Calgary, Alberta; **13.3** iStockphoto (Christopher Futcher), Calgary, Alberta; **13.4** iStockphoto (Catherine Yeulet), Calgary, Alberta; **14.1** Thinkstock (Lifesize), München; **21.1** Thinkstock (iStockphoto), München; **24** www.CartoonStock.com (Delgado, Roy), Bath; **25.1** NEWSTEAM/SWNS Group (Mathew Growcoot), Bristol; **25.2** Picture-Alliance (dpa/epa), Frankfurt; **25.3** Thinkstock (Comstock), München; **26.1** shutterstock (Poznyakov), New York, NY; **26.2** shutterstock (Monkey Business Images), New York, NY; **27.1** Getty Images (Peter Dench), München; **30.1** dreamstime.com (Lucian Milasan), Brentwood, TN; **31.1** Corbis (Kulka), Düsseldorf; **33.1** AMAZON by Bruce Parry (Michael Joseph 2008) Reproduced by permission of Penguin Books Ltd.; **33.2** iStockphoto (Marisa Allegra Williams), Calgary, Alberta; **37.1** www.CartoonStock.com (Chris Madden), Bath; **37.1** Mauritius Images (Alamy), Mittenwald; **39.1** shutterstock (Fotomicar), New York, NY; **39.2** shutterstock (-Albachiaraa-), New York, NY; **43.1** Corbis (Charles O´Rear), Düsseldorf; **43.2** Picture-Alliance, Frankfurt; **44.1** Fotolia.com (Ayupov Evgeniy), New York; **46.1** Getty Images (Philip Ryalls/Redferns), München; **48.1; 48.2; 48.3; 48.4** Klett-Archiv, Stuttgart; **49.1** Zapiro, Kapstadt; **50.1** shutterstock (dean bertoncelj), New York, NY; **50.2** Corbis (Nigel Pavitt/JAI), Düsseldorf; **51.1** Mauritius Images (Alamy), Mittenwald; **51.2** Alamy Images (Greg Balfour Evans), Abingdon, Oxon; **57.1** iStockphoto (Lisa F. Young), Calgary, Alberta; **58.1** iStockphoto (RonTech2000), Calgary, Alberta; **58.2** iStockphoto (kristian sekulic), Calgary, Alberta; **59.1** Fotolia.com (photolifepnw), New York; **59.2** iStockphoto (Kevin McKeever), Calgary, Alberta; **60.1** Corbis (Barry Lewis/In Pictures), Düsseldorf; **61.1** iStockphoto (Janne Ahvo), Calgary, Alberta; **62.1** Fotolia.com (Antonie Graumann), New York; **62.1** Klett-Archiv, Stuttgart; **63.1** Mauritius Images (Alamy), Mittenwald; **65.1** www.CartoonStock.com (Hardin, Patrick), Bath; **65.2** www.CartoonStock.com (Carpenter, Dave), Bath; **67.1** iStockphoto (Brian McEntire), Calgary, Alberta; **76.1** iStockphoto (Jonathan Heger), Calgary, Alberta; **76.2** Fotolia.com (wiw), New York; **76.3** iStockphoto (Kurt Bertels), Calgary, Alberta; **76.4** Fotolia.com (Marcel Hurni), New York; **77.1** iStockphoto (Claudia Dewald), Calgary, Alberta; **78.1** iStockphoto (Özgür Donmaz), Calgary, Alberta

Sollte es in einem Einzelfall nicht gelungen sein, den korrekten Rechteinhaber ausfindig zu machen, so werden berechtigte Ansprüche selbstverständlich im Rahmen der üblichen Regelungen abgegolten.

Textquellennachweis
S.5 Extracts from *Emma*, by Jane Austen; **S.33-34** © Extracts from: Bruce Parry 'Amazon', © Penguin Books Ltd., London; **S.74** © Guardian News & Media Ltd. 2009

Green Line Oberstufe Klasse 10
ISBN: 978-3-12-560021-8

CD-ROM

Empfohlene Systemvoraussetzungen:
Betriebssysteme mit Webbrowser ab:

- Microsoft Internet Explorer 5.5, Mozilla Firefox 2.0, Safari 3.0, Opera 9.0, Konqueror 3.2
- PC: Pentium 166 MHz
- Mac: 400 MHz, G3 PowerPC oder Intel-basierter Macintosh Computer
- CD-ROM Laufwerk
- 512 MB RAM
- Grafikkarte 24 Bit Farben
- Soundkarte
- Adobe Reader ab Version 5, Adobe Flash Player ab Version 9

Auf der CD-ROM befindet sich ein ausführliches Handbuch zum Programm.

Mündliche Prüfungen: Vorbereiten, prüfen und bewerten

Green Line Oberstufe
Klasse 10 Mündliche Prüfungen mit CD-ROM

Vorschläge für mündliche Prüfungen mit methodischen Hinweisen zur Vorbereitung, Durchführung und Bewertung.
Mit Lösungsvorschlägen und Erwartungshorizonten, perforierten *Role Cards* zum Herauslösen und editierbaren Materialien auf CD-ROM.

Kopiervorlagen mit CD-ROM: ISBN 978-3-12-560099-7

Nützliche Materialien für Ihre Schülerinnen und Schüler

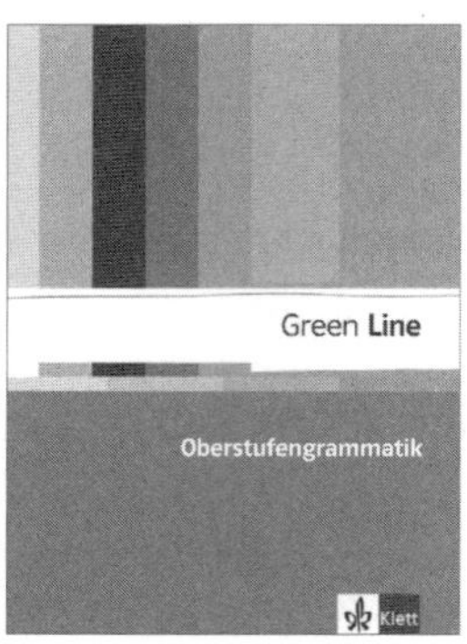

Green Line
Oberstufengrammatik

Grammatik mit genau den Inhalten, die in der Oberstufe verlangt werden. Einfache Regeln und Erklärungen auf Deutsch machen die Grammatik klar und verständlich. Sie ist speziell ausgerichtet auf Fehlervermeidung und auf die Bewältigung aller sprachproduktiven Aufgaben der Oberstufe. Unterteilt in Grund- und Aufbauniveau, funktional und kontrastiv angelegt; mit vielen Tipps. Das dazu passende Arbeitsheft eignet sich ideal zum Vertiefen und praktischen Anwenden der Grammatik. Die CD-ROM enthält Lösungen bzw. Erwartungshorizonte zu allen Aufgaben sowie Kommentare und Hilfen zur Selbstevaluation.

Nachschlagegrammatik: ISBN 978-3-12-595501-1 • Arbeitsheft: ISBN 978-3-12-595502-8

Green Line Oberstufe Kl. 10
Vokabeltraining aktiv

Viele zusätzliche Wortschatzübungen passend zum Schülerbuch Green Line Oberstufe Kl. 10 unterstützen die Schülerinnen und Schüler beim Vokabellernen – besonders beim Schreiben der neuen Vokabeln. Mit allen Lösungen zum selbstständigen Überprüfen.

Arbeitsheft: ISBN 978-3-12-560031-7